How to Love Yankees
Yankees
with a Clear Conscience

How to Love Yankees
with a Clear Conscience

BO WHALEY

Rutledge Hill Press
NASHVILLE, TENNESSEE 37210

To **Donna Rae** —
  A Yankee by birth
  a Rebel by choice,
  and one of the finest
    to migrate South from Chicargo, Illernoise.
Thanks to her,
  I learned to love a Yankee
  ... with a clear conscience.

Copyright © 1988 by Bo Whaley

Published in Nashville, Tennessee, by Rutledge Hill Press, Inc., 211 Seventh Avenue North, Nashville, Tennessee 37219

Library of Congress Cataloging-in-Publication Data

Whaley, Bo, 1926–
    How to love Yankees with a clear conscience/Bo Whaley,
        p.   cm.
    ISBN 0-934395 77-2
    1. Northeastern States — Social life and customs — Humor. 2. Southern States — Social life and customs — Humor.   I. Title.
PN6231.N693W5 1988
818'.5402 — dc19   88-15799
                                                                              CIP

10 11 12 13 — 96 95 94
Manufactured in the United States of America

INTRODUCTION

April 9, 1865, is the day the American Civil War ended, when General Robert E. Lee surrendered the Army of Northern Virginia to General Ulysses S. Grant at Appomattox Court House, a little place about seventy miles west of Richmond. The end of the war? Yes. The end of the hostilities? Hardly.

There are hordes south of the Mason–Dixon Line who maintain that the war was misnamed to begin with and that it should properly be referred to as The War Between the States, The War of Yankee Agression, or The War For Southern Independence. Some still argue—either in South Georgia juke joints or New York taverns—that it was really the War Between the Good Guys and the Bad Guys. Where you come from determines which side is which.

Such an argument reportedly took place in a Brooklyn, New York, bar several years ago between a native New Yorker and a visitor from South Carolina.

"Shucks," said the South Carolinian, "we could'a whupped y'all with cornstalks."

"Oh, yeah? Well, why didn't you'se do it, eh?" asked the New Yorker.

"Because y'all wouldn' fight with cornstalks, tha's why!"

Then, there is the legendary story of the Yankee who was attending a convention in Atlanta and became very depressed. He decided to commit suicide by jumping from a high floor of one of the city's downtown hotels.

"Watch out! I'm going to jump!" he yelled from high above the lobby.

"Wait! Don't jump!" yelled a man in the crowd that had gathered in the lobby below. "Think about your wife and children!"

"I don't have a wife and children! I'm going to jump!"

"No! Don't jump! Think about your mother and father!" the man yelled back.

"I don't have a mother and father! Watch out! Here I come!"

"Wait! Please don't jump! Uh . . . think about Robert E. Lee!" the man down below called up in desperation.

"Robert E. Lee?" the would-be jumper said. "Who the hell is Robert E. Lee?"

"What?" the man in the lobby exclaimed in disbelief. "Well, go ahead and jump you Yankee SOB!"

And so it goes.

But this book was not designed, and is not intended, to settle the many differences inherent to the sons of both north and south. No doubt the Blue–Gray arguments will continue forever, or at least as long as athletic teams from both regions face each other on the field or in the arena and those from both sides of the Mason–Dixon Line sit side by side on bar stools, gulp beer, watch the action on television, and root for the home team.

This book is my attempt to shed some light on the lifestyles and cultures of both Yankees and Rebels and to foster tolerance and understanding among them. I'm convinced that Yankees ain't all bad, just a little peculiar perhaps, and they talk funny, as you will see.

I hope this book will prove invaluable to my Rebel friends who take the plunge and travel to such places as Detroit, Newark, and New York. By reading here they will at least have a vague understanding of how Yankees talk, what they're eating, and why everybody up there is always in such a hurry. After spending fifteen years in the North, I never figured out whether the natives are runnin' to somethin' or from somethin'.

Another thing. Everybody in New York—from a first grader to a Wall Street broker—carries a briefcase, and I always wondered what was inside 'em. I'm convinced that a New Yorker could no more walk straight without a briefcase than some of my friends down here could walk straight without a tackle box and a reel and rod, or a gallon jug.

Hopefully, this book will serve as a vehicle to lay to rest

some of the many misconceptions harbored in the minds of both Rebels and Yankees about each other. Not everybody in Yankeeland talks like Archie Bunker; likewise, those of us in the Southland don't all talk like Andy Griffith. I say this only because one of the big communication barriers on both sides of the famous dividing line has always been language. While English is the dominant language, we don't all speak it with the same dialect.

Probably one of the biggest shocks of my life came when I touched down on foreign soil—Detroit—for the first time in 1955 and came face to face with the language barricade. I was well into 1956 before learning that a babushka wasn't an implement used to cut weeds, a novena wasn't a small town in South Carolina, a scarf wasn't the first half of Al Capone's nickname, "Scarface," a union was something other than a marriage between man and woman, and a strike-breaker wasn't a pinch hitter for the Detroit Tigers. I also learned that Canada is not in Europe and that snow, while pretty and white, is also slushy and messy.

While I sincerely hope that reading this book will prove to be fun, I also try hard in here to lay out early on some of the many misconceptions concerning our Yankee brothers by those of us born and raised in Dixie.

If there is a general purpose associated with the writing of this book, it has to be this: to shed light where there's been mostly only heat. A Southerner can no more learn about the life and cultures of Yankees by taking a three-day visit through Michigan, New Jersey, Pennsylvania, and New York than can a Yankee by motoring south through Tennessee, South Carolina, and Georgia en route to Florida.

Indeed, the Northern heritage and its roots aren't to be fully determined by touring an automobile plant in Detroit, climbing to the top of the Empire State Building, or taking a Circle Line Tour around Manhattan in New York City, stopping in a South Philadelphia bar for a beer, or riding the New Jersey Turnpike.

Neither is the southern culture to be learned by touring the Jack Daniel distillery in Tennessee, stopping off briefly at a gift shop in Dillon, South Carolina, or visiting Herb's Reptile Farm and House of Prayer on the outskirts of Ludowici in South Georgia.

Travel brochures won't help much, either. You have to eat, live, and sleep the region for a while. You have to smell it, get to know its people and how they live and worship. Really, it's akin to being in prison or having a baby—you have to experience it to really know what it's like. I did, spending fifteen years in Michigan, New York, and New Jersey. Now I'm hard at work on my forty-fifth year in Dixie. Take it from one who's been on both sides of the Mason–Dixon fence: there are a bunch of good folks on both sides.

I am a Southerner, a proud Southerner. I live and breathe the Southland and constantly give thanks to God for the good life those of us who live here enjoy. But I recognize the contributions made by Yankees in the past to our southern culture and its traditions, one in particular: the Southland's national anthem, "Dixie." What? That's right. The song came to us from "up yonder," New York.

I have strong thoughts and sentiments about this grand old song, and I disagree with those who regard it as racist. "Dixie" is not—nor was it ever intended to be—racist. Still others say the song is offensive. Not me.

I find "Dixie" to be no more racist or offensive than other regional songs, like: "New York, New York," "Chicago," "California, Here I Come," "I Left My Heart In San Francisco," "Alabama Jubilee," "Tennessee Waltz," "Carolina Moon," "Chattanooga Choo-Choo," "The Eyes of Texas Are Upon You," "Back Home in Indiana," and "Oklahoma."

And what about "Detroit City," "Way Down Yonder in New Orleans," "By the Time I Get to Phoenix," "Birmingham Jail," "Kansas City, Here I Come," "Rainy Night in Georgia," and "Take Me Back to Tulsa?"

Racist and offensive? I think not.

I go all the way back to near infancy with "Dixie." I've been rocked to sleep by it, awakened by it and marched to it. Take a look at the words and see if you find this song racist or offensive:

> I wish I was in the land of cotton, old times there are not forgotten, Look away! Look away! Look away! Dixie Land.
> In Dixie Land where I was born in, early on one frosty morning, Look away! Look away! Look away! Dixie Land.

(*Chorus*)

Then I wish I was in Dixie, Hooray! Hooray! In Dixie Land I'll take my stand, to live and die in Dixie. Away, away, away down south in Dixie. Away, away, away down south in Dixie."

(And do you know there is a second verse?)

There's buckwheat cakes and Injun butter; Makes you fat or a little fatter. . . .

Then hoe it down and scratch your gravel; To Dixie Land I'm bound to travel. . . ."

I ask you, what's racist or offensive about that?

Here are a few little known facts about "Dixie" that you might find interesting. Did you know that:

- The song was written (in 1859) in New York City?
- The man who wrote it, Dan Emmett, was from Ohio?
- Emmett also wrote "Turkey in the Straw" and "Blue Tailed Fly"?
- At the age of fifteen he wrote "Old Dan Tucker," using his own name (Dan) and that of his old dog (Tucker)?
- Emmett was, himself, a true Union man?
- The original first verse was discarded because Emmett's wife disliked it for the verse's irreverence (in her eyes)? Here it is:

Dis world was made in jus' six days; And finished up in various ways. Look away—look away—look away, Dixie Land!

Den dey made Dixie trim and nice; An' Adam called it Paradise; Look away—look away—look away, Dixie Land!

Also, did you know that:

- At President Lincoln's Inaugural Ball the night of March 4, 1861, the music for the Lincoln Grand March was none other than Daniel Emmett's "Dixie." According to *The New York Times* of March 5, 1861, "Patriotic airs were generally played . . . 'Dixie' was a great favorite with anyone who knew what a good tune was."
- On April 8, 1865, after having paid a visit to battered and burned-out Petersburg, Virginia, President Abraham Lincoln and his party were saying goodbye to the war zone. Steaming up the Potomac River aboard the Riverboat Queen, Lincoln was asked by the leader of the military band aboard what numbers he would particularly like to hear. Lincoln requested

but two: "The Marseilles" and "Dixie." They proved to be his last musical requests. He was assassinated five days later.

So you already have learned something about the South that may be a surprise to you. Hopefully this book will contain much more that's new to you—about both the North and the South.

You can't really love or hate anybody with conviction unless you know them. Hearsay won't work. It ain't even admissable. But you can hang your hat on this: It is possible to love Yankees with a clear conscience. Even with the blood of the South coursing through your veins!

CONTENTS

11

SECTION ONE

HATING YANKEES AIN'T A CREDIT COURSE

YOU CAN'T LOVE 'EM IF YOU DON'T KNOW 'EM

Contrary to popular belief in many sections of the North Country, those born and raised below the Mason–Dixon Line are not taught from their youth up to hate Yankees. It just flat ain't true.

I was 27 years old before I first set foot on foreign soil, New York City, and I can tell you with authority that I never knew or heard of anyone in my home state of Georgia touring the South with a tent to preach the evils of Yankeedom. Oh there still are those diehards who keep fighting (and losing) the Civil War with regularity. Their arguments come and go, but the end result of that War For Southern Independence never changes: Lee surrendered to Grant at Appomattox on April 9, 1865, and the South began to pull itself up by its bootstrings.

In my early childhood in deep South Georgia I well remember that there were a few scattered Yankees around, but they were considered in the same light as illegitimate babies and ex-husbands: while you knew they were around, you just sort of ignored 'em. As far as I was concerned, they were harmless, as long as their number remained small. A little obnoxious and pushy, yes, but not really a threat to the southern lifestyle.

Some of the older folks had set ways about Yankees and wouldn't budge on the question. I knew a boy whose Mama whipped him good because he sat by a Yankee in the local picture show, and there was the case of another who was invited to visit his "ahntie" in Detroit. Every youngster in the South has an "ahntie" in Detroit, and before he left the boy's Daddy made him get inoculated by old "Doc" Garrison who was a combination General Practitioner and Veterinarian with an office in the back of the feed store.

"Can't be too careful," said the boy's Daddy. "Shoot 'im with everything you got, Doc, an' then dip 'im. I don't want the boy goin' off up yonder an' ketchin' somethin' then bringin' it back heah an' givin' it to my cows an' hogs."

Just such reasoning, or lack of it, is precisely what prompted my writing this book, coupled with a fifteen-year observation of the folks in Michigan, New York, New Jersey, and Pennsylvania. Most of the pre-conceived notions harbored by Southerners and Northerners about each other just ain't true.

If those of us in Dixie are to love Yankees, we must first know something about them. That is my philosophy. We can neither hate nor love anybody with authority unless we understand them.

PRECONCEIVED NOTIONS
SOUTHERNERS HAVE ABOUT YANKEES

Here are some preconceived notions Southerners hold about those living north of the Youse–Y'all dividing line. Since most of these ideas are untrue, it is important to get them out into the open. Such ideas are:

- That everybody north of Baltimore is suspect.
- That all women living in the Bronx have hairy legs and eat garlic for breakfast every morning. (One true son of the South even went so far as to say that "the most effective form of birth control is a Bronx accent." Just not totally true, Beauregard. The garlic has to be a contributing factor.)
- That every man over the age of 18 in New York is a member of the Mafia.
- That lifelong residents of Brooklyn think Atlanta is located just over the Brooklyn Bridge somewhere in the vicinity of the Holland Tunnel.
- That California is a member of the United Nations.
- That there are continuous race riots in Detroit around the clock. Both sides riot in eight-hour shifts and are members of Race Rioters and Headbusters Local 609.
- That it snows year round in Michigan, and the sun only comes out on July 4th.
- That the only religion in Philadelphia is Catholicism.
- That everybody in New York goes to the ball park on Sunday afternoon. They sit in the bleachers, remove their shirts, drink beer, get sloppy and abusive, and curse the umpires. Not true. Some of them do not sit in the bleachers.
- That people in New York City actually live in telephone booths and public rest rooms. Also not true.

Some have no roof over their heads at all, and there is a waiting list for telephone booths and public rest rooms.

• That cold-water flats (apartments) rent for as much as $1,000 a month. This is obviously in error. I have a good friend who lives in one, and he pays $1,500 a month.

• That everything in the North is overpriced. Probably. But there is one constant in both North and South: a fella' can still get five pennies for a nickel. The last time I visited in New York (July, 1985) I had a cup of coffee in my hotel, gave the cashier a $5 bill, and received $3.25 in change. I kept standing there with my hand out. He asked me what my problem was. "No problem," I said. "I'm just waiting for the deed to the restaurant." He had no sense of humor whatsoever and mumbled something that sounded like "Hick."

• That every nightclub and restaurant is filled to capacity with television, movie, and Broadway stars. Not true. I stayed in the city for five nights, and the closest I came to seeing a star was the visiting team batboy from Yankee Stadium at the Bronx Zoo and a Go-Go Dancer who performs at Nudie Rudy's Skin Ranch in Times Square as she stepped out of a taxi and ran inside a side door to Nudie Rudy's. From the scant amount of clothing she was wearing, I think she was ready to perform when she arrived. I know she was either wearing a short skirt or a wide belt, but I'm not sure which, I just know that based on what I saw, or didn't see, a moth would starve to death in her clothes closet.

• That a large segment of the population of Brooklyn drink beer from the time the bars open at 7 A.M. until closing. This is another misconception of Yankees. Heck, some bars in Brooklyn don't open until 7:30 A.M.

• That every socialite in New York City has a poodle. Not so. Some have cats, and one I know has a jaguar.

• That Newark is a suburb of New York City. I don't know exactly what Newark is. I worked in the city for six years and, frankly, I'm convinced there ain't no reason for it to exist.

• That all Yankees eventually retire to the South. This is only partly true. Only those who can find The South retire here.

PRE-CONCEIVED NOTIONS YANKEES HAVE ABOUT SOUTHERNERS

Here are some equally wrong ideas Northerners have about those living south of the Youse–Y'All dividing line. These ideas hold up to scrutiny about as well as some of those Southerners have about Yankees. As you can see, I've added a few corrections of my own.

- That Southerners talk funnier than they do.
- That all women in the South are in the kitchen, barefoot, and pregnant. Not anymore. Some spend a lot of time in the den.
- That moonshine is the regional drink and is served at all wedding receptions. This can't be true. If it were, the groom would never be able to back out of the drive-way and get on with the honeymoon.
- That the majority of southern men spend most of their time hunting and fish-ing. I don't know a lot about that, other than that it takes almost as much time to scale fish and clean birds as it does to catch 'em and kill 'em.
- That all southern girls fourteen years of age and over are married. Ridiculous! I know a bunch in that age category who just shack up.
- That every man, woman, and child in the South owns a coon dog, a cat, or a frog.
- That grits grow on three-inch trees and are picked by midgets from Ringling Broth-ers during the off-season.
- That there really ain't no such thing as buttermilk. Sure is! It comes from a but-ter cow, and if your stomach looks anything like the glass it is downed from after it dries—heaven help you!
- That "Dixie" is sung at all weddings and funerals and is the official song of "Designing Women."

19

• That everybody down South talks with a drawl and sounds as if he or she is chewing homemade biscuits or boiled peanuts.

• That Southerners eat clabber as a substitute for yogurt.

• That mules are extinct.

• That Jack Daniel invented whiskey.

• That Atlanta Opera performers sing country songs.

• That hardly anybody down South watches "The David Letterman Show" that originates from New York. Well, more people would watch it if it wasn't on opposite "The Soybean Report" and "How to Whittle While the Mash Ferments." Priorities, you know.

• That Archie Bunker ain't a hero in the South. Wrong! He's right up there with Andy Griffith.

• That Sunday afternoons are spent mostly sitting under a giant magnolia tree, drinking mint juleps. Most Southerners outside of Louisville, Kentucky, ain't never seen a mint julep, and most of the giant magnolias have long since been cut for pulpwood along with all the other trees.

• That a man has two prized possessions—his bird dog and his wife—and prays long and hard that he'll never have to make a choice between them. While he can always stick something frozen in the microwave, it's just hard to find a wife who'll hold a point or retrieve quail.

SECTION TWO

A REBEL IN YANKEELAND

YANKEELAND ENTRANCE EXAMINATION

For the benefit of my southern brothers, let me caution you that there is more to a Yankee invasion than loading up the ol' pickup, having the ole lady fry up a batch of chicken, filling the cooler with longneck Buds and RC Colas and the gas tank with regular, stashing the young'uns and the dog in back and heading North. A trip there, whether for a temporary visit or—God forbid—to take up permanent residence, requires some planning.

First and foremost, you must by all means attend the fish fry or barbeque given for you by the neighbors to celebrate your departure because your journey into the never-never land of the cold country may well be the biggest thing to happen in your hometown since the mass liquor still raid in 1968, the one that produced the big wedding. Remember? The deputy sheriff and the daughter of the revenue man who led the raid? Not many towns of 2,500 can boast of a having had a formal wedding in the basement of the county jail, with trusties serving at a reception that featured Vienna sausage, saltine crackers, RC Cola punch, moon pies, beef jerkys, pigskins, grits dip, and rat cheese.

Like the immigration station located just north of Dillon, South Carolina, that processes Yankees heading south, a similar one awaits unsuspecting Southerners with a northern destination. It is located on the outskirts of Baltimore, Maryland, not far from the Chesapeake Bay Bridge, and is financed by an annual grant from the U.S. Congress. It is a union shop with all personnel recruited from Michigan, New Jersey, New York, and Pennsylvania, the policy being that no one who ever traveled south will be considered for employment.

The oral examination administered there really ain't all that bad, provided you can understand what the girl asking the questions is saying. But that problem can be overcome with a telephone call and twenty-five dollars; there is an interpretation service in Baltimore staffed by a team of mixed breeds, those who have spent considerable time in both north and south. The telephone number is on the walls of both the men's and women's rest rooms located behind the immigration station and the fee is twenty-five dollars cash—no credit cards—to interpret for the duration of the oral examination. (Be sure and get a receipt because the fee is fully deductible, but only on state income tax forms in states located south of Maryland.)

The written examination is another ball of wax. You'll be on your own with this one. I failed it on my first two tries but passed by the skin of my teeth the third time around after being tutored for ten days by a traveling salesman from Long Island, New York.

Here are some of the things you should have at least a general knowledge of before you embark on your journey:

- You should know the basic difference between a deli, a doily, and a dolly.
- You should know that any mention of a cab in Manhattan is in no way a reference to a pickup truck or a tractor–trailer rig.
- You should know that any mention of a borough in New York City is in no way a reference to a small donkey or a jackass.
- You should know that the Empire State Building is not the governor's mansion or the home of the New York City mayor.
- You should know the general sale price for the Brooklyn Bridge.
- You should know to omit any questions calling for a general summation of the activities of the Mafia, especially if the guy giving the test is named Genovese, Gallo, Gambino, Luchese, or Luciano.
- You should know the names of at least one Italian restaurant in New York City. Mama Leone's will do.
- You should know that it is not true that Madison Square Garden has to be fertilized once a year.
- You should know that a Broadway play is not an end around or a power sweep in-

cluded in the New York Giants' playbook.

• You should know that in Chicago when a guy tells you to "go to El," he isn't being disrespectful or insulting, but merely telling you how and where to catch a train.

• You should know that nobody really lives in New York City; they just work there. They really live in New Jersey and Connecticut.

• You should know that there is activity in Times Square year-round, not just on New Year's Eve.

• You should know that reservations are required for everything you do in New York City, even going to a pay toilet.

• You should know that people in New York City don't live next door to one another, but rather on top of each other.

• You should know that when mufflers are mentioned, in most cases reference is being made to a heavy scarf worn around the neck for warmth. It has absolutely nothing to do with the thing dragging behind your pickup.

• You should know that Saint Patrick's Cathedral is *not* the home of Auburn University football coach, Pat Dye.

• You should know that the Pan Am Building has absolutely nothing to do with the Panama Canal.

• You should know that "four-in-the-floor" has a decidedly different meaning in New York City than it has in Waycross, Georgia,

THE LANGUAGE—WHAT YOU HEAR IS WHAT YOU GET

One of the first things I noticed when I moved north was that folks up there talk funny. Even little kids. It is very possible to mix and mingle for hours in a room with Yankees of all ages talking a mile a minute and have no idea what's being said, unless you have done your homework.

Inasmuch as this is a self-help book, designed for the purpose of assisting unsuspecting Southerners visiting in such places as New York, Detroit, and New Jersey, I have compiled a glossary that should prove invaluable. Naturally, the longer the visit, the more words that will be added to the list. But for starters the fifty words listed here should at least get one in and out the door and possibly help in avoiding embarrassment.

Under no circumstances should an innocent Southern visitor make an attempt to repeat vocally what he hears while rubbing elbows "up yonder." It simply won't come out right and, besides, it is impossible to adapt to a foreign language on a short visit.

For your assistance and convenience, the Yankee spelling of each word is followed by the correct spelling of the word in parentheses. Then there will be an example of how the word can be used in a sentence.

It is strongly suggested that this section of the book be clipped and saved for ready reference when backed into a corner and no earthly idea is forthcoming as to what is being said. These words are by no means a complete listing of the Yankee vocabulary, but rather key ones to have at your disposal.

Should those with whom you chance to be mixing and mingling at the time wander off into a verbal dissertation that strongly resembles a debate in the United Nations, move back to the hors d'oeuvre table and proceed to stab little sausages with toothpicks until the conversation returns to as normal a level in English as a Yankee conversation can get.

I distinctly recall having attended a reception in New Jersey where I mixed and mingled for most of a Saturday afternoon before enjoying a delicious meal consisting of dishes I couldn't pronounce with people I couldn't understand. My only successful communication was with the man seated on my right. On one occasion I said, "Please pass the salt," and later he countered with, "Please pass the pepper." I would have traded my snow shovel and thrown in a loaf of pumpernickel to have had access to just such a Yankee glossary as I am going to give you now.

And remember, **NEVER LEAVE HOME WITHOUT IT!**

Word	How It's Used
Gedouddaheah (Get out of here):	I'm fed up with your coming in late smelling of beer and cheap perfume. Just pack up your junk and gedouddaheah!
Whassamattayou (What is the matter with you?):	Loan you ten bucks when already ya' owe me twenty? Whassamattayou? Ya' crazy or somethin'?
Broad (Woman; girl; female):	Boy! Dat wuz some broad I seen ya' wit las' nite.
Fodder (Father):	Angelo says his Fodder can whip your Fodder.
Mudder (Mother):	Oh, yeah? Dat may be, but I'll bet his Fodder can't whip my Mudder.
Goil (Girl):	No doubt about it, Louie; dat Marie is da uglies' goil in P. S. 39. (P. S. 39 is a public school.)

Lorr *(Law):*

My son, Herbie, was gonna' go to Harvard an' study medicine but he changed his mind and went to Yale to study lorr.

Earl *(Oil):*

Yeah, gimmee' five bucks worth o' super unleaded an' check the' earl.

BOIL with EARL

OIL with BERLE

Oil *(Earl):*

Hey, Oil! While you're checkin' da earl how 'bout checkin' da batt'ry wadah.

True *(Through):*

Are ya' believin' dis? Da traffic was so bad dis mornin' it took me more'n ten minutes ta' git true da' Lincoln Tunnel.

Tree *(Three):*

Ya' say ya' wanna' git ta' where? Flatbush Avenue an' Roosevelt? No problem, go tree lights up an' turn right.

Wit *(With):*

Jus' park your car, Dominick, an' you'se can ride wit me.

Hoi *(Hi!):*

Hoi, gois! Are you'se goin' to da' poker game at Ricco's?

Goi *(Guy):*

I seen dat play at da teeater las' nite, "Gois and Dolls." Great!

Erster *(Oyster):*   Nah, can't make it to da union meetin' t'nite, Salvatore. Me'n Margie's goin' over ta Hubuken (Hoboken) an' eat some ersters an' guzzle a few at th' Clam Broth House.

Boid *(Bird):*   Dem Knicks don' stan' a chance. Da Celtics will eat 'em alive. Dat Larry Boid is da greates' dere is.

Joisey *(New Jersey):*   Yeah, I work at Staten Island but I live ovah in Joisey. (Never New Jersey).

Terlet *(Toilet):*   Hello, Louie? Dis is Archie. Kin ya' git ovah ta my house right away? My terlet is stopped up.

Shoit *(Shirt):*   Hey, Marie! What'd ya do wit my bowlin shoit after ya ironed it?

Lawn Gyland *(Long Island):*   Yea, Freddie, it's been good livin' in y'r neighborhood here in da Bronx, but me'n Hazel's movin' out. Bought us a place on Lawn Gyland.

Foist *(First):*   Hey! Whattayatalkin? My Gran'mudder can play foist base beddah dan dat bum!

Tanks *(Thanks):*   I'd rilly like ta go wit'cha to da races, Paul, but I made other plans a'ready. Tanks anyway.

Coib *(Curb):*   Can you imagine what dat stupid kid o' mine done? Took my car an' went speedin' down da Lawn Gyland Expressway an' jumped da coib. Hit a guy on a bicycle an' two joggers.

Fort *(Fourth):*   Know what Danny's teecher done? Da dumb broad flunked him an' now he's gotta' repeat da fort grade.

Toity Toid *(Thirty-third):*   Yeah, I been workin' out f'r th' las' tree munts at da Toity-Toid Street gym.

Trow *(Throw)*: I wuz talkin' ta Oinie's (Ernie's) pop las' nite an' he says da kid is gonna' sign wit da White Sox. Da kid kin rilly trow a baseball. Benny says he's been clocked at 98 miles per hour.

Single; Fin; Sawbuck; C-Note; Yard *($1; $5; $10; $100; $1,000)*: Hold it a minute, Jack, and let me step in the bank and get some change an' I'll put some green on ya. Two folks I always pay, my bookie an' da ol' lady's alimony. I need 12 singles, tree fins, a C-note, five sawbucks and four yards— $4,177. (Money Line: From what I gathered they have their own currency and money language in the Big Apple.)

Dis *(This)*: Well, I'll jus' tell you dis sport. Dis is a helluva' way ta run a railroad.

Dem *(Them)*: How da ya' like dem apples, huh?

Dat *(That)*: Ya can believe dis, George: Dat tie don' go wit dat suit.

Doze *(Those)*: It jus' ain't grammatically right ta say dem peoples, Sid. You s'pose ta say doze peoples.

Day *(They)*: Mama, I took da chicken soup to da Farenchello's house like you said, but day wasn't home.

Turteen *(Thirteen)*: I'll lay ya two ta one dat dere wasn't but turteen original states when America was created.

Tink *(Think)*: Well, I still tink dere was 14. How 'bout Brooklyn?

Taught *(Thought)*: I taught dere was 14, too, but Jimmy the bartender at Max's showed me a beer bottle what proved dere was jus' turteen.

Awriteareddy *(All right, already)*: Awriteareddy! I'm comin'! I'm comin'!

Den *(Then):*   O.K., Maria—first you cook the ground beef in a separate pan over medium heat. Den, you stir in the canned tomatoes and two pounds of garlic.

Duh *(The):*   Eddie, run down to duh deli an' tell Mr. Cohen to send me tree pounds of liverwurst.

Lotsa *(Lots of):*   I'd like a pepperoni and mushroom pizza, with lotsa mushrooms.

Donju *(Don't you):*   Donju leave this house till I get back!

You'se *(You all):*   You'se guys wait till I git back an we'll go muggin' in Central Park.

Piece *(Gun):*   I never go near Central Park 'less I'm packin' my piece.

Oily *(Early):*   I'm goin' ta Rosie an' Luigi's weddin' an' then stop by th' reception f'r a few minutes, but I have ta leave oily. Dis is da nite I watch rasslin' on TV, an' I don' miss that f'r nuttin'.

Witcha *(With you):*   Hey, Rocco! When you drive over ta Joisey t'morrer, can I go witcha?

Sawr *(Saw):* — I taut I sawr ya downta' Hoibie's dis mornin'.

Drawering *(Drawing):* — Hey, Marie! Whatcha drawerin' in dat colorin' book?

Potty *(Party):* — Can't make it, Joey. Me'n duh ol' lady is goin' to a Noo Yeer's Eve potty at Rafael's.

Doit *(Dirt):* — Trow a li'l doit in dat hole, Benjie, an' le's go tuh Angelo's f'r a beah.

Cuber *(Cuba):* — I tell youse whut I say; to hell wit Castro an' Cuber.

Avnoo *(Avenue):* — I'll meetcha' at Barney's on Flatbush Avnoo.

Moitle *(Myrtle):* — Moitle an' Oil (Earl) is gittin' married at St. Luke's t'morrer.

Berld *(Boiled):* — My ol' man says dat Khadafy oughta' be berld in earl.

Soitainly *(Certainly):* — Whaddayatalkin? Soitainly I'm goin' tuh da Gients' game.

Champeen *(Champion):* — I seen Joe Louis fight in duh Garden twice't when he was duh hevvyweight champeen.

Chiner *(China):* — I wudeen take dat broad out in public f'r all duh tea in Chiner.

Consoined *(Concerned):* — I'm consoined 'bout Oinie. He don' look right.

Emmer *(Emma):* — I tell youse whut I tink. Dat Emmer Bombeck is a funny lady.

Poil *(Pearl):* — Didja' hear 'bout dat bum, Oil? He found a poil in 'is erster.

Nize *(Noise):* — Nah! I ain't buyin' no diesel cah. Makes too much nize.

Pok *(Park):* — Seen duh papuh dis mornin'? Two

more bums got dere's in Central Pok las' night.

Nuttin' *(Nothing):* Nuttin' doin', fella'. I ain't messin' wit no lottry.

Woids *(Words):* Ya' took duh woids right outta' my mout'.

Wantchas *(Want you):* I wantchas all tuh meet me in da Bronx brew'ry in da' mornin'.

Pitcher *(Picture):* Did'ja see dat pitcher o' Rombutello in duh *Times* dis mornin? Hard tuh reconize wit all dem bullet holes in 'is cheeks.

Choich *(Church):* I hoid dey foun' "Li'l" Joe behin' de choich ovah on Toity-Toid wit 'is neck broke.

Disere *(This here):* Wait a minute! Do it like disere.

Noospapuh *(Newspaper):* Yeah, I seen it in duh noospapuh.

Aintment *(Ointment):* Da skin ain't hardly broke. Jus' tell yer mommer tuh put a liddle aintment on it.

Cah *(Car):* Youse guys go on in an' git us a good seat while I pok duh cah.

Stiff *(Corpse):* Serves da stiff right fer gittin' caut in da ack. Dey's buryin' 'im dis afternoon in St. Bahneventure's.

Puss *(Face):* Frankie let 'im hol' one right in da puss an' laid 'im out col'.

Kisser (Same song, second verse).

Laig *(Leg):* Th' way I figgerit, he ain't got a laig tuh stand on. Guilty as sin, plus he's got hissef a crappy mout' piece.

Mout'piece *(Lawyer):* See above.

Joik *(Jerk):*   Gedouddaheah! Da guy's a joik!

Bah *(Bar):*   Boy! Did I evah get smashed las' night! I stopped in at Bennie's Bah intent on havin' a couple, but I run inta' dat broad who's da featured strippah at Georgie's Strip n' Clip on Broadway an' we ended up at her place in Joisey. Wow! Fum dere it wuz light's out 'til dis mornin'.

Pleece *(Police):*   I seen da pleece cah wit duh lamp burnin' and duh wissel blowin' but I figgered it wuz jus' another cop late f'r lunch at Oscar's.

Dine *(Dying):*   Some train wreck las' night, huh? People dine all ovah duh place.

Figgah *(Figure):*   Did'ja see dat broad wit Kenny at duh fights las' night? Wow! Some figgah! Makes dat Dolly Parton look anemic, huh?

DO'S AND DON'TS FOR Y'ALL

Relocating can be a frustrating experience, and there is more of it going on now than ever before. Some are making permanent moves north while others are merely going for a look-see to satisfy their curiosity and then returning home to talk about it. It matters not the reason behind the travel; there are still many things relating to culture and lifestyles that just should and shouldn't be done once your intended destination has been reached.

For instance, a Southerner journeying north for the first time should refrain from instructing a New York cab driver on the intricacies of driving in Manhattan. Likewise, a Northerner venturing south on his maiden voyage should never say to the owner of a South Georgia juke joint, "Well, that ain't the way we done it in Joisey." In the first place, New York cab drivers drive like no other drivers in the world so any helpful hint will fall on deaf ears. In the second place, South Georgia juke joint owners don't really give a damn how anybody does it in Joisey.

The innocent and unsuspecting Southerner bent on taking a trip to the big city "up yonder," will soon see for himself if all he's heard about Yankee country is true. Most make their virgin voyage to New York City, and if they survive they venture out to other such outposts as Detroit, Newark, Boston, Philadelphia, and maybe Chicago if the wind has died down. These Do's and Don'ts will prove invaluable, and some of them may well save your life.

Do Not

• Take your pistol with you to New York. It ain't legal because of the Sullivan Law, which prohibits guns there. You see, they have a funny thing going in New York about guns; the only people allowed to have them are the Mafia and lesser crooks who pay the police.

• Take a casual stroll through Central Park unless you are flanked by Arnold Swartzenegger and Paul Bunyan. The Central Park Muggers are organized and do shift work. They all belong to Muggers Local 8910 and strike every day and night—any and everybody they can accost. They do take credit cards and anything else you have on your person.

• Visit Harlem on a sightseeing tour with your wife, Frieda May. And for goodness sake don't take your little girl, Kay, with you if you ignore my advice and take Frieda May there anyway. But if little Kay squalls and cries to the heavens that she wants to go along, too, be sure you hold her hand tight because should she wander off and get lost while you're looking at the sights and reading all the graffiti spray-painted on the buildings you'd be in one heck of a fix. Why? Hell, man, you'd have more company than a multi-millionaire uncle on his deathbed if you suddenly cupped your hands around your mouth and began yelling, "Kay! Kay! Kay!" at the top of your voice.

• Even consider buying a "genuine" Rolex from the guy you'll meet in the vicinity of Broadway and 42nd Street—and you *will* meet him—who has watches strapped on both arms from his wrists to his armpits. The going price for an Oyster Perpetual in legitimate Rolex outlets is roughly $2,800. The Presidential, a solid gold model, kicks off at somewhere in the neighborhood of $12,000, and that really ain't a bad neighborhood. The New York street vendor will slide one or both off his arm for about $30 and $85 respectively. And he has genuine diamonds, mounted and unmounted, in a little plastic bag secreted in his pocket, probably the same little plastic bag his cocaine came in and which he bought within minutes following his last sale. His diamonds go cheap. Heck, for $100 he'd probably sell you the Hope diamond and throw in Elizabeth Taylor, depending on how badly he needs that cocaine.

• Miss taking the wife and Kay on the Circle Line Tour around Manhattan. It's one of the few genuine bargains to be found in New York City.

• Leave anything unlocked, and if you can figure out a way to get your pickup in your hotel room, do it! Remember. For every tourist coming into New York wearing jewelry and carrying money, there are ten hoodlums trying to figure out the best way to steal it or take it away from you.

• Buy anything with the label cut out or the serial number deleted. If you do, that's an excellent way to meet and get on a first name basis with one of the city's 20,000 finest—a New York City policeman.

• Ride in a taxicab. But if you find it necessary to do so, take two things with you inside the taxicab: a bountiful supply of Valium and an interpreter. They drive like a bat out of hell and speak no English. I don't see how there can possibly be anybody left in Haiti, Cuba, Guatemala, Spain, Portugal, the Dominican Republic, or Puerto Rico. They're all in New York driving taxicabs.

• Be a smart-ass and approach some guy wearing dark glasses, an expensive Italian pin-stripe suit, a white-on-white shirt, a loud tie, a pinky ring, a real Rolex watch (Presidential Model), over-the-calf socks, and black Italian shoes with toes so pointed you could thread a needle with them and say, "Hey, Cuz . . . kin ya' tail me whurabouts that Mafier bunch hangs out at?" You do, and that would be the appropriate time to say goodbye to Frieda May and little Kay. You see, that bulge under his coat ain't no beeper. They deliver their messages in person, and they're *always* on call.

• Commit the unpardonable sin of telling Polish jokes in any Hamtramck, Michigan, bar, or Italian jokes in Grosse Pointe. Both situations could be hazardous to your health.

• Take a swim in the East River. While many do, they don't do it intentionally. Besides, it's awfully hard to do the breaststroke while wearing two cement blocks on your feet with your hands tied behind you.

• Accept any offer from a Broadway and 42nd Street female to accompany her to a sleazy hotel room for "a good time." This, also, could be hazardous to your health. A good ole boy from North Alabama can vouch for that. He responded after being told by one of the bright light ladies that if he'd accompany her she would "wind his watch." Back in the big city two years later, the same female approached him with the same sales pitch as before. The sicker but wiser Alabama native politely declined, saying, "No thank you, m'am. You wound it when I wuz heah two years ago an' it's still runnin'."

• Ever go to a porno movie and sit on the back row or to a wrestling match in Madison Square Garden and sit on the front row. You do and folks in the city will know a lot about you right off.

• Ride a subway train unless absolutely necessary. If you do, put your hands in your pockets to protect your money. But don't be surprised if you find another hand got there before yours.

• Make up the bed in your hotel room before checking out. There are two basic reasons for this: there are maids employed to perform this service and they belong to Bedmaker's Local 4032. Believe me, they'll report you to the shop steward, and he carries a baseball bat and brass knuckles.

• Leave less than a two dollar tip for any waiter after any meal. They have a way of quickly sizing your ability to pay up and are experts at spilling hot coffee in your lap and hard rolls on your head, with both being hazardous to your health. Remember this: matire' d' types and waiters run New York and other big city restaurants. The owners merely count the money.

• Go to anything in New York without reservations. You will find that no matter what you decide to do or where you decide to go, at least 100,000 other folks beat you to it.

• Order grits at Mama Leone's. There's no way you will be forgiven for it.

Do

• Put your money in your shoe before you get off the bus at the Port Authority Building.

• Identify your next of kin and "person to be notified in case of emergency" in writing and leave a copy with the undertaker, your lawyer, and your preacher before boarding the bus in Montgomery. Remember: it's better to be safe than sorry.

• Eat a sidewalk cart hot dog while in the city. There are none better.

• Avoid walking on Park Avenue. Ask Dan Rather about it. Just remember that millions of poodles, merely an extension of their owners, walk there daily and leave evidence that they've done so. Walking on Park Avenue and attempting to avoid poodle droppings is like playing hopscotch. I always entertained the delightful fantasy of witnessing a horse poo-poo on Park Avenue and then standing back to watch a rich poodle step in it.

• Attend a Broadway play, even if you do have to mortgage the farm, float a loan on the house, and wait in line from Groundhog's Day until Thanksgiving to buy tickets.

• Go to the top of the Empire State Building. It is the best vantage point from which to view the mass hysteria down below known as the New York rush hour. The city resembles a giant ant bed from up there, and the view probably inspired the author of this best-selling bumper sticker: "The Rat Race Is Over—The Rats Won!"

• Stand for a little while on any street corner in Manhattan and ponder. This is when you will give thanks for the privilege of living in East Texas, North Alabama, or South Georgia.

• Arrange a visit to the Statue of Liberty. One native son of Tennessee did on the final day of a five-day visit to New York and was overheard mumbling this to the Lady with the Torch: "I'll just tell ya', m'am. If you ever plan to see this ol' boy agin, you flat gonna' have to turn around."

• Send bushels of postcards to the folks back home so they can sit around and say, "What in th' world is Bubba' doin' up there? He lost his mind 'er somethin'?"

• Buy a round trip ticket.

TO MOVE OR NOT TO MOVE

I've just seen the results of a Chase Manhattan Bank Survey regarding naming the ten best, and ten worst, states to retire to. I've either lived, worked, or visited in all of them. Here's what the survey showed:

The ten best states to retire to:

1. Utah
2. Louisiana
3. South Carolina
4. Nevada
5. Texas
6. New Mexico
7. Alabama
8. Arizona
9. Florida
10. Georgia

The ten worst states to retire to:

1. Massachussetts
2. Maine
3. New Jersey
4. Vermont
5. Rhode Island
6. New York
7. New Hampshire
8. Connecticut
9. North Dakota
10. Minnesota

I find it revealing that nine of the ten best states to retire to are all below the Mason–Dixon Line, and the ten worst are above it. Food for thought?

O. K., here are the fifteen places I'd least like to live and the fifteen places I'd most like to live . . . if I had to leave Dublin, Georgia.

THE FIFTEEN PLACES I'D LEAST LIKE TO LIVE:

1. *Atlanta, Georgia.* I wouldn't have minded living there back when it was a Southern city. Not now. I don't want to live in no city where more residents eat potatoes than grits for breakfast, and where tee times have to be reserved.

2. *Miami, Florida.* I draw the line at homesteading in any city where I'd need an interpreter.

3. *Boston, Massachussetts.* No thank you. I think it would be terribly degrading to have the natives reach for my wrist, look at their watch and take my IQ before engaging in conversation with me.

4. *Albuquerque, New Mexico.* I think I would enjoy the people, but I balk at moving into any city where I have to enroll in night school to learn how to spell it.

5. *Washington, D.C.* Can you imagine living in a city where everybody came from someplace else and is either a consultant, a lawyer, or sucking the federal sugar teat? Washington is the padded cell of America.

6. *Hilton Head Island, South Carolina.* No thanks, I don't want to live no place where everybody's favorite pastime is tryin' to impress everybody else.

7. *Baltimore, Maryland.* Forget it. I don't want to sign on with no state what don't know if it's north or south.

8. *Minneapolis/St. Paul, Minnesota.* The way I figure it, Mary Tyler Moore ain't there no more, and I can't think of no other reason to move in.

9. *New York, New York.* If you've ever been there, you'll know why; if you ain't, you wouldn't understand. The only way I would consent to living in New York would be with a guarantee that I could live next door to Archie Bunker.

10. *Butte, Montana.* I ain't about to pick up and move to a figment of the imagination. Ludlow Porch, Atlanta radio dynamo, says there ain't no such place as Montana, and if Ludlow says it, that's good enough for me. By the way, have you ever actually met anybody from Montana?

11. *Newark, New Jersey.* Can you imagine living in any city where the cleanest street is the one leading to and from the city dump?

12. *Dallas, Texas.* Only place I've ever been where everybody thinks they're better than everybody else. Dallas needs to take lessons from Fort Worth in how to live.

13. *Salt Lake City, Utah.* I just have the feeling that all the defrocked television evangelists are gonna' flock to Salt Lake City one day, sell their Rolex watches and Lincoln Town Cars, build an "Evangel Dome" about twice the size of the Pentagon, and take over the world.

14. *Morgantown, West Virginia.* While I give the state the benefit of the doubt and accept the fact that it is out there somewhere, I ain't never had nobody verify it.

15. *Coeur d'Alene, Idaho.* Same as #4.

THE 15 PLACES I'D MOST LIKE TO LIVE:

1. *Fort Worth, Texas.* See #12 above.

2. *Port St. Lucie, Florida.* This is the best kept secret in Florida, and J. C. Hillary's may just be the best restaurant in Florida. Great seafood!

3. *Detroit, Michigan.* Detroit, Michigan? Right. I spent seven great years there. I like the people and the city. Plus, there are so many Southerners living there and working in the automobile plants that it's no trouble to find a restaurant (cafe) that serves grits.

4. *Guadalajara, Mexico.* This may be as close to paradise as a man can get. The city has all the pluses, and very few minuses. Temperature? A delightful 72 degrees most of the time.

5. *Kingston, Ontario, Canada.* Beautiful! And what could be wrong with any country that gave us Ann Murray and Paul Anka?

6. *Hershey, Pennsylvania.* The cleanest city I've ever seen. The food is great, and so are the people. Plus, all that chocolate!

7. *Watertown, New York.* What a shame it is that the mere mention of *New York* immediately produces a vision of congested city streets, around-the-clock crime, and

a daily struggle just to survive when New York State is one of America's most beautiful. A picture post card photographer would be in hog heaven in this state.

8. Savannah, Georgia. Just my favorite city in America, that's all. I don't have room to tell why.

9. Birmingham, Alabama. Like great food, pretty women that know how to dress, and a city where every citizen is a self-appointed ambassador of good will for the chamber of commerce? That's Birmingham.

10. Highlands, North Carolina. God worked overtime in creating Highlands. I'd love to live there, but I can't. I don't have a winter home in West Palm Beach, Florida, a pre-requisite.

11. Nashville, Tennessee. I tried it once and I loved it. And there's a lot more to it than the Grand Ole Opry.

12. San Diego, California. Guadalajara with a zip code! I've lived there, and would go back in a wink. It's the best thing California has to offer.

13. Seattle, Washington. The queen of the Northwest, a beautiful city. Plus I love to drink coffee, read and write when it's raining.

14. Mackinaw Island, Michigan. People search all their lives for a place like this. The Grand Hotel is in a class by itself. And there are no cars allowed. It's either walk or ride a bicycle. You go there and leave by ferry or sled. Only the policeman has a car, and I always wondered: who jumps his car off when it won't start on cold mornings?

15. Hendersonville, North Carolina. I've been vacationing in Hendersonville since early childhood. My Daddy knew a good thing when he saw it. It's as close to nature as a person can get.

GETTING READY TO GO NAWTH

I'm telling you it would be a disaster for the virgin traveler or transplant to go north without making the necessary preparations. It would be like throwing a piece of raw beef into a dogpen filled with pit bulldogs.

To help the adjustment, I've put together some suggestions that can make the adjustment easier, and probably prevent a lot of serious embarrassment. Bear in mind, now—These are only the basics.

SUGGESTIONS FOR SOUTHERNERS MOVING NORTH:

• Call your local radio station or place a classified ad in your local newspaper to try and sell your peanut scoop. Then put the money in your sock so you can buy a shovel.

• Go to the local stock car speedway and practice jumping between the cars as they speed around the track. This will come in handy while dodging taxicabs every morning in New York as you walk to work after getting off the commuter train. Playing hopscotch in a fire ant bed for several weeks will also prove helpful.

• Learn to eat hardrolls on the run for breakfast the way the Yankees do. If you can find a small piece of granite or marble to chew on for practice, it will help.

• Try and adjust to reading your morning newspaper folded about four or five times until it is about the size of a small paperback book. Learn to turn it from front to back with one arm extended above your head. This procedure will stand you in good stead on the subway inasmuch as space, even a few inches of it, is precious in New York.

• Go to the local high school and run with the track team, concentrating heavily on the dashes and low hurdles. The extra speed you'll generate will come in handy in New York, especially if your plan is to spend any time in Central Park. The hurdles will condition you to sailing over the bodies of those in Central Park who preceded you but made no such advance preparation.

• As often as possible before departing for the north country, stand in line at such places as banks, supermarkets, football stadium rest rooms, giveaway food lines, and lines to purchase tickets to rock and country music concerts. This will prepare you for the lines in which you'll spend a major portion of your time in New York and New Jersey because up there you'll learn quickly that no matter what you decide to do over the weekend, at least a million people had the same idea—and before you.

• Write to the AFL–CIO for information regarding labor unions, almost nonexistent in the deep South.

You will be amazed to learn that unions have absolutely no relation to marriage, and a union suit ain't really a pair of underdrawers featuring a trap door in back but a grievance filed in court against the company that pays your salary. Also, Local 15 is not a reference to the train that passes through town every morning around 3 A.M., with its whistle blowing at every crossing—both of 'em.

• Go ahead and accept the fact that up north you're probably going to be living upstairs—way upstairs—like thirty or forty stories upstairs. And that you don't just "step outside" and go to the corner grocery for cigarettes.

• It would be a good idea for you to invest in a weekend trip up north—to Atlanta—and spend some time riding elevators in a few of the hotels and office buildings. Much time is spent on elevators in northern cities. Babies have been born on elevators, some whose mothers never made it off the elevator from the time the baby was conceived until birth. Like I said, space is precious and privacy is all but impossible in New York City.

• Commuting is another thing you need to know about. If you will be required to clock in at 8 A.M. once you've relocated to the city, it would be well for you to go to pick out a spot on the river from which it will take you roughly an hour-and-a-half to two hours to drive to your present job and pitch a tent. Then, for a couple of weeks, set the alarm and get up at 4:30 A.M. in order to get ready and make it to work on time. This is what happens in millions of households every morning in Yankeeland.

• If you can, try and find some "All in the Family" re-runs on your television set and watch 'em. This show will portray life in New York City for the working man as closely as anything you'll find, and you'll love Archie Bunker. The man is flat out, genuine, Bronx.

• Go to your local supermarket and load up on frozen dinners featuring such Yankee standards as Spanakopita (Spinach Pie), Vichyssoise, Ratatouille, Chicken Cacciatore, Quiche Lorraine, Vitello Tonnato, and Veal Francais. Learn to pronounce and eat them. I realize they sound subversive and/or Mafia related, but take my word for it, they're legal and Yankees really eat 'em. You might as well go ahead and get used to 'em 'cause such delicacies as Chicken and Dumplings, Sweet Potato Pie, Crackling Bread, Heavenly Hash, Country Ham, and Country Sausage are nonexistent "up there."

● While in Atlanta riding those elevators, take a break now and then to walk up and down Peachtree Street at a fast pace; look straight ahead and don't speak to nobody. Try to develop a far away look in your eyes, like you might be in a trance. It's called the "New York" look. During World War II in the South Pacific, I saw the same look on soldiers who'd been there for three or four years. It was called the "Asiatic Stare." And while you're at it, roll up a newspaper and stick it under your arm. Try to look important and intelligent.

● Get in your car at the peak of the Atlanta rush hour traffic and try to get to I-75 and I-285 from downtown. It will take somewhere in the vicinity of three hours. Be sure and blow your horn often and change lanes every chance you get. If you can negotiate Atlanta traffic, Manhattan will be a breeze.

● Seriously consider scrapping the whole idea of moving north and stay where you are. Compared to the city traffic, commuting, long lines, and foreign food, the gnats ain't really all that bad.

BIG CITY LIVING IS FOR THE BIRDS

During the final round of the last golf tournament in Dublin, I was riding the course with a doctor friend. It was just a perfect day. Suddenly, on the twelfth fairway, he stopped his golf cart, turned to me, and said, "Bo, you know, we're mighty lucky to be living in Dublin."

I endorsed his thought a hundred percent. City life? I want no part of it. I had a shot of it in Washington, Houston, Detroit, Newark, and New York for fourteen years, 150 of 'em commuting from New Jersey to the Asphalt Jungle. It's called the rat race. I guess it's like pulling a hitch in the Army, you'd hate to have missed it but would hate like the devil to have to repeat it.

Take a look at the rat race as they live it up north with me, then pause and thank God you live and work here.

Here's the picture as I see it. It happens every day.

It's 6:30 A.M. You are confronted by a monster in the bathroom mirror. He glares back at you like one of the hundreds of Red Chinese infantrymen who spent most of the night marching across your tongue wearing muddy combat boots. Happiness is a tube of toothpaste, and there it is! On top of the commode tank, with the cap missing. And it has oozed and it's crusty. The heck with it. Where's the Lavoris?

It's cold and rainy outside, and it's Monday. You vaguely contemplate suicide while shaving but decide against it after nicking your ear lobe, uncapping a gusher. A home remedy, toilet tissue, is applied but keeps falling off.

A vain attempt is made to get dressed with one hand, the other affixed to your right ear lobe, oozing O-

47

positive. And, a button is missing from your oxford cloth button-down, the same button that was missing last Monday morning. You hang it back in the closet, eyeing the .38 revolver on the dresser. It'll hang there, buttonless, until you sleepily drag it out again, probably on another rainy and cold Monday morning when you're running eight minutes late or the Monday after you forgot to move the clock ahead one hour in April.

"She," in hair rollers, is her usual cheery self as she places two sunny-sides before you, one with the yolk broken, which prompts you to wonder if she is suffering from a hormone deficiency, or something. Her logic is ill-received when she mutters a faintly audible "it had to be broken sooner or later." (Translation: "If you don't like the way I cook 'em, then cook 'em yourself!") Years of similar mornings have taught you to squelch your response.

Still at the table, you observe through a rain-spattered window that John Dillinger Jr. has managed for the fourth consecutive morning to shred your *New York Times* while delivering same through, not around or over,

her prized rose garden. Your thoughts desert the eggs and revert momentarily back to the dresser and the .38 lying there. The thought of Wednesday's headline quells your contemplation.

"Suburban Sniper, Father of Two, Murders *Times* Delivery Boy!"

No jury composed of commuters would ever convict you.

Your concentration is suddenly shattered when, from the remote environs of the upstairs bedroom, the sound of barely controlled chaos ruptures your eardrums as a door is flung open wide and the ear-splitting sounds of "Boston," "The Grateful Dead," and "Grand Funk Railroad," emit therefrom. Hide the pistol!

Enter your two adolescents. Which one is the girl? The one you assume to be collapses in a chair without so much as a civil "good morning" and mumbles through her hands that she simply *must* have a new fall. What the heck is a fall? Through careful cross-examination you determine that it is some sort of hairpiece and *everybody* is wearing one and they're on sale for only $29.95!

Not having time to give

your summation regarding the fall, Junior, practically lying on the table, dabbles at his oatmeal while fingering a broken guitar string. His lips resemble a Zulu witch doctor as he informs you that his R-string is broken and he has to have one tonight.

Unconditional surrender is the price of peace and up goes the white napkin. Out comes the checkbook. Fastest draw this side of the. . . .

But wait! Ladybird comes to life just long enough to inform you that it will be necessary to invite one of those members of the Mafia to come take a diagnostic look at the washing machine. And, the warranty expired last Thursday! Boy, this is where the action is. No doubt about that.

On your way out to the garage, you ignore the fact that the morning light has crowned all that is about you with the beauty of a new day. Chirping birds and dancing sun rays are wasted on you this Monday morning as you prepare for the second leg of the rat race. At this point, you are behind. You see only 11,000 clams worth of sleek status, sculpted in steel and decorated in leather and chrome, with initials on the door, yet.

There it is, your personal projectile, in partnership with David Rockefeller and Chase Manhattan. It's your entry in the daily rat race, and it zooms as you pull out of your drive and head it for the coastal highway, with a tissue-covered right ear lobe.

Missing toothpaste caps, busted buttons, broken egg yolks, shredded newspapers, falls, R-strings, and that darned washing machine. You've had it. Today, without fail, you'll march right in and discuss it with the boss. The Anti-Poverty Program . . . yours!

In an effort to by-pass the morning migration into the city, you exercise your option and take the masochistic route, the freeway. Once on it, the ocean is to your immediate right. It's been there for over a zillion years and will be there for a zillion more. Anyway, you've seen it already. Every day. Twice. Out where the sea and sky hold hands white sails propel a sailboat to an unknown destination. But, it goes unnoticed by you in the mania to "get there." You are doing your thing. You are a participant in the daily rat race.

Got to keep abreast of the times. Civic duty and all that

jazz. Can't do that with a shredded newspaper. You solve that with just a touch of the radio button that brings forth a nonsectional but too-happy voice for such an early hour to apprise you of the state of the world with the morning news.

First, there's discrimination in housing, equal employment opportunity, quickly followed by urban renewal, air and water pollution, busing and educational guidelines, public transportation, and a defeated bond issue. And, don't forget to vote.

The radio voice drones on, throwing in a dash of Project Head Start, the war on poverty (which catches your ear), beautify America, and labor relations. Next comes price-wage guidelines, air-rail-shipping strikes, and a Mafia murder in a Brooklyn barber shop. (You lean forward in anticipation. Was the victim a washing machine repairman? No luck. The nonsectional early riser tells you that he was a narcotics dealer.)

Then, Congressional committees and committees to investigate committees. Man! One thing about government. We sure got a heck of a lot of it! (Surely the puppeteer must inevitably strangle in his own strings.)

Time out for the eleventh

commercial during this news update. You are approaching the Lincoln Tunnel as the sexy voice tries to sell you a package of cigarettes. She's a mile and a half late. You light your pipe in protest. You've had enough. The same button that turned them on turns them off. Click!

Your mind wanders as you creep through the tunnel, well aware of the asphalt jungle awaiting you at the exit. Suddenly, for no reason, you realize that you're eighteen minutes early. Enough time for a tranquil cup of coffee and a glance at an un-shredded newspaper.

You exit and the ocean looks great spread out like a giant front yard with sky-scrapers in the background. And, isn't that a pretty sail-boat out there slipping along? A portrait of peace and tranquility. You steal yet another glance before turning on 40th Street to drive to Madison Square Garden and park your projectile before starting on the last leg of your race to survive the frus-trations of city life, the rat race.

You exit the parking garage, enter the subway train and jostle toward 69th Street, along with a few thousand other rats. You somehow feel like the one that got caught in the trap and said, "To heck with the cheese, I just want out!"

You resign yourself to the fact that if you are to buy falls, R-strings, shredded newspapers, broken eggs, and pay washing machine repairmen—not to mention your own personal projec-tile—you'll simply have to run in the rat race every day until you find the end of the rainbow. Dixie!

And, you're right, my friend. We're mighty lucky to be living here.

NEW YORK—THERE'S NO OTHER PLACE LIKE IT

I hadn't ridden a train since the late 1960s, and here it was the summer of 1985. I figured I was overdue, plus the fact that I hadn't been in New York in 25 years. I took the plunge and boarded the Silver Meteor in Savannah on a Sunday night and settled in for an overnight ride to the big city, with a short stop in Washington.

Three newspapers, "dinner in the diner," and "ham and eggs in Carolina" later, I debarked at Pennsylvania (6–5000) Station and hailed one of New York's 11,000 taxis, thereby instantly becoming a bonafide tourist as well as a Yellow Cab daredevil.

There's a lot to be said about riding trains, like a train is the only land-based machine in which a man can walk drunk while sober or walk sober while drunk. Of course, after my arrival I saw some people on the streets of New York that performed both feats simultaneously.

I saw a man walking on a public street in the shadow of the Empire State Building decked out in a suit coat and a pair of Fruit-of-the-Loom underdrawers, nothing else. And he was singing "Amazing Grace." Nobody afforded the guy a passing glance. The guy could have been wearing a chartreuse turban and yellow sneakers and it would have caused no more concern. Only in New York.

I ask you, where else but in New York would you witness these everyday occurrences?

- It starts to rain at 2:25 P.M. and at 2:27 P.M. the street hawkers have set up sidewalk shops and are selling umbrellas.
- An aged, over-the-hill boxer jogging in the middle of Broadway decked out in boxing gloves and shadow boxing with an imaginary

opponent every third step, and winning.

- A pair of Chinamen squatting on the sidewalk on 48th Street with mobs of people walking by and around them, playing checkers and oblivious to their surroundings.

- Signs on Manhattan parking garages all over advertising bargain rates—six hours for "only" $12.50.

- Bumper-to-bumper taxis at war with bumper-to-bumper pedestrians, thousands of horns blowing to no avail.

- Office buildings that disappear into the sky—or somewhere.

- Hundreds of thousands of people walking to or from somewhere and staring straight ahead.

- Smartly dressed women, wearing expensive dresses, rushing frantically at 5 P.M. wearing sneakers and carrying their expensive high heels in their hands, trying to make it to the bus or subway.

- Two cab drivers arguing furiously, one speaking Spanish and the other Italian, neither having any earthly idea what the other one is saying—but both are saying it loudly.

- Horses pulling surreys on Park Avenue while block-long limousines honk loudly for them to move over. The horses win.

New York. It is a city of tall buildings and short money.

LABOR UNIONS CAN IMPRESS ALL AGES

Those of us born and raised in the South know very little about labor unions. I guess the main thing we know about them is that industry flees from them at every opportunity—usually to the South—and that almost everything and everybody in the North is unionized.

My first knowledge of labor unions came when I moved to Detroit in 1955. I mean, you don't get nothing done there without union approval. Do you think that the automobile workers who make your cars work for Ford, General Motors, and Chrysler? No way! They work for the union, and what the union says goes. If the union says, "Knock off at 3:37 P.M.," then not another bolt, screw, nut, or washer will be installed after that time.

Contracts are big with unions. If the contract spells it out, you do it or get it. If not, forget it.

This story was making the rounds when I lived and worked in Detroit:

It seems that a nine-year-old boy came home from school one afternoon, dropped his books on the sofa, made himself a sandwich and yelled to his mother that he was going outside to play. This in itself was no cause for alarm, but the fact that it was well after dark when he returned home was. Naturally, his mother demanded to know where he'd been, what he'd been doing and why he missed dinner. And when a nine-year-old boy misses dinner, that is indeed cause for alarm.

"Just where have you been and what have you been doing, young man?" his mother asked.

"Been over at that new

subdivision back of the school," he replied.

"And just what were you doing there?"

"Been learnin' how to build a house," the boy said as he reached for a cold piece of roast beef and a slice of bread.

"Oh yeah? Well, just tell me what you learned about building a house," his mother ordered.

"Well, for one thing I learned how to hang a door," the kid said nonchalantly.

"And just how *do* you hang a door?"

"Takes two men to do it," he said. "One man takes the door and holds it in place while the other man backs off 'bout twenty steps and yells at him—'Move the damn thing 'bout three inches to the left!'"

The mother was flabbergasted, but soon regained her composure and asked, "Well, what *else* did you learn about house building?"

"Learned how to hang a window."

Cautiously, his mother asked, "How is *that* done?"

"Well, the two men trade places. The one that yelled at the man holding the door goes up and holds the window while the one that was holding the door backs off 'bout twenty steps and yells back at him—'That's good! Stick a nail in the bastard to hold it and let's get the hell out of here and go get a beer! It's quittin' time!'"

His mother almost dropped her potholder as she turned to face the boy. "Such language I never heard from a nine-year-old! You just march outside and bring me a switch, young man!"

The boy looked up at his mother with nothing but contempt in his eyes and said matter-of-factly, "A switch? Go get your own damn switch, lady! I ain't no electrician, I'm a carpenter!"

YANKEE LIFESTYLES CAN BE TRAUMATIC

For the Southerner traveling north on vacation for the first time, there are some real eye-openers sure to impress and provide conversation topics for months after returning home. There are the skyscrapers of New York City that seem to reach into infinity. There are the automobile factories in Detroit and its environs where a visitor can take advantage of the opportunity to see firsthand how automobiles are assembled. Niagara Falls is beyond comprehension. The Empire State Building, Radio City Music Hall, Rockefeller Center, The Statue of Liberty, Broadway, Chinatown, and hundreds of other phenomenons ensure the tourists of both an educational and fun-packed vacation.

On the other hand, there are things to be seen in New York City that the folks back home will have difficulty understanding or believing. Like some of the nightclubs, prices, New York cab drivers, the subway system, the Automat, Times Square, and many, many more.

Here's an example of an almost unbelievable experience as related by Charlie Joe Bentley, a good ol' boy, upon returning home to Albany, Georgia, from the Big Apple. He traveled to New York for the very first time at age forty-seven after having won a vacation trip there for being the leading fertilizer salesman in his company. He told the gang in his hometown about one unique experience in a New York nightclub named "Lavender and Chartreuse." This was his story:

After repeated efforts to gain admission to "Studio 54" without success, he sauntered into Lavender and Chartreuse, in Greenwich Village, where no reservation was required. His

manner of dress—a conservative suit—immediately branded
him as a tourist, an outsider.

"Shoot! I seen things in that place I never knowed existed,"
Charlie Joe told the boys between sips on a longneck Bud.
"Like boys with lavender hair and chartreuse fingernails as
long as a Pall Mall."

"Ya' mean that, Charlie Joe?" asked a bug-eyed "Bubba"
Boatwright.

"If I'm lyin', I'm dyin. Unbleevable."

"Whut ailse, Charlie Joe?" asked "Buster" Martin.

"Well, I paid eight dollars to git in an' so help me I didn'
walk six steps 'fore I run right up on two boys holdin' hands
an' gigglin'. An' in a booth ovah in a dark corner behind 'em
I seen two more with their arms 'round each other, jus' a'
huggin' away hard as they could go."

"You plumb sure they's boys, Charlie Joe?"

"Sure as you're born! An' I seen two more all huddled up together on a sofa behin' a flimsy curtain, but the lavender smoke comin' fum th' dance floor wuz so thick I couldn' see whut it was they wuz doin'. I do know one of 'em had on high heel shoes an' the other'n wuz a' wearin' danglin' ear-rings."

"Whut'd ya' do, Charlie Joe?" asked "Buster."

"Well, I jus' sort o' moseyed 'roun f'r a little while an' watched," said Charlie Joe. "Then, I got out on the dance floor and wuz dancin' away when I seen somethin' that'd make a wrestler throw up."

"Whut! Whut'd ya' see?" asked "Bubba."

"Well, I know you ain't gonna' bleeve this, but right out there on the dance floor in front o' God n' ever'body they wuz two boys jus' standin' there kissin' each other!"

"You don't mean it?' said an unbelieving "Buster."

"Sure as you're born! I seen it with my own eyes. It was downright disgustin' to me. I thought I wuz gonna' thow up right there on the dance floor."

"Whut'd ya' do, Charlie Joe?" "Bubba" and "Buster" asked in unison.

"Whut'd I do? I'll tell ya' whut I done. I wuz so disgusted I jus' walked right off'n that dance floor an' left the boy I wuz dancin with standin' there!"

SECTION THREE

A YANKEE IN REBELLAND

DIXIELAND ENTRANCE EXAMINATION

While I have never seen it, I understand there is an immigration station just north of Dillon, South Carolina, near the North Carolina line. I have it on good authority that it was built shortly after World War II and has been operational since 1949. Its purpose is to process Yankees bent on moving South.

The personnel who man the station are carefully selected, a prerequisite being that they be direct descendents of a Confederate soldier who served honorably and with distinction in the War of Yankee Aggression. Until his retirement in 1985, Beauregard P. Lee commanded the station and was replaced by Thomas J. ("Brickwall") Jackson who is now in charge.

The South Carolina immigration station is financed by a ten percent surcharge on all moonshine whiskey made in South Carolina, Georgia, and North Carolina, and since its opening in 1949 there has never been a shortage of funds.

Several years ago a friend of mine from Detroit, Michigan, retired after thirty years on the assembly line at Ford's River Rouge Plant, considered his options, and wisely chose to spend his retirement years in North Florida. Like hundreds of thousands of others had done before him, he bought a condominium and headed south. But he encountered one major obstacle: he almost didn't pass the Dixieland Entrance Examination given to all Yankees moving South at the South Carolina immigration station.

"It was rough," he said. "I spent three days at a motel near Dillon, South of the Border I think it's called, and took a refresher course called 'Southern Is As Southern Does' in an abandoned warehouse in Hamer, South Carolina, not far from

Dillion. I told 'em at the immigration station that I had a great uncle from Sumter who fought on the side of the South, and a great-grandfather who was born, raised, and died in Waycross, Georgia, and who was for years a Justice of the Peace. That didn't make no difference. I still had to take the immigration test, and pass it, before being cleared to go further South."

So, in order to make things easy for those planning to retire and head South, let me clue you in on some of the basics that you should at least have a talking knowledge of before arriving at the Dillon immigration station and sitting down to take "the test."

- You should know the basic differences between Missionary Baptists, Free Will Baptists, Hard Shell Baptists, Primitive Baptists, and Foot-Washing Baptists. (And it wouldn't hurt none to brush up on what is Pentecostal and what ain't.)
- You should know the difference between a hissie fit and a conniption fit.
- You should know the difference between a tick and a blue tick.
- You should know the difference between a second cousin and a first cousin once removed.
- You should know where Rock City is.
- You should know at least the first verse of "Dixie."
- You should know the hometown of Flannery O'Connor.

- You should know the difference between "seerup" and "sirrup."
- You should know approximately how many fish are in a mess.
- You should know the difference between sour mash and bourbon.
- You should know at least one place where a fella' can buy a moon pie and an RC Cola in the same store.

- You should know approximately how long boiled peanuts should be boiled.
- You should know the price that Number One hogs and soybeans brought yesterday.
- You should know the difference between a bottom plow and a middle buster.
- You should be able to explain just exactly what "catty-cornered" and "cattywampus" mean.
- You should be able to name the entire cast of "The Andy Griffith Show."
- You should know these dates: When Lee surrendered at Appomattox; When the Grand Ole Opry was founded; When and where *Gone with the Wind* premiered; When Atlanta sold out to the North; When the Georgia–Florida game will be played this year; When the South rejoined the Union.
- You should know at least two recipes for biscuits, one for sweet potato pie, one for chicken and dumplings, one for hoecake, one for banana pudding, and none for chitlins.
- You should know the approximate location of Ludowici, Georgia, and you should know to slow down when you drive through.
- You should know the name of one Southerner who lives at Sea Island and one who lives at Hilton Head. If you have difficulty, make a long distance call to the chambers of commerce in each place. They might know if such a rarity exists.
- You should know what "stump juice" is.
- You should know what "pot likker" is.
- You should know the difference between a "boar" and a "sow." And between a "heifer," a "bull," and a "steer." (You can bet your passport they do.)
- You should know the sum total of forty 'leven dozen.
- You should know what a "bush bond" is.
- You should know the difference between "prefab" and "double-wide."

If you reach the point where you have at least a working knowledge of the above, you should have no difficulty passing the immigration test and proceeding on to your southern destination.

Good luck, and rest assured that you will be welcomed with open arms in Dixie.

DO'S AND DON'TS FOR YOUSE

R elocating to the South can be as frustrating for Yankees as heading north often is for sons and daughters of the South. Like Southerners, some Yankees make permanent moves while others merely go for a look-see and return home to tell their neighbors what happened. Like their southern counterparts, traveling Yankees need to know these many things relating to culture and lifestyles that just should and shouldn't be done once they've arrived at their destination. It isn't enough to know how they do it in Boston or Chicago. When in Rome . . . . You know the rest.

To those who plan to move south from the frigid north country after donating your snow shovel and mittens to the children, bear this in mind: If your ultimate destination is Atlanta, Georgia, and your plan is to live there permanently, then forget or completely disregard everything suggested for your group that is designated for Yankees. It won't apply, because upon your arrival in Atlanta from New York City you won't be able to tell the difference (with the possible exception of the weather). Atlanta is a little warmer in winter but about the same in summer.

Atlanta, you see, was once a southern city. But that was before the northern industry with its northern money discovered it sometime in the mid-1950s. You will no doubt feel right at home in the Atlanta traffic, especially during rush hours. Natives of the South avoid it like the plague and wherever possible enlist sharecroppers and other underlings to travel to Atlanta and do their bidding. Reports abound of some who have made the trip and never returned, the contention being that they are still circling the city on Interstate

285, the 67-mile monster that encompasses the city under the guise of being a bypass.

It is documented that one Major League baseball pitcher, Pasqual Perez, failed to show up and take the mound for the Atlanta Braves at Atlanta–Fulton County Stadium because of a major difficulty on I–285. The young man simply couldn't figure a way to exit the monster and, coupled with the fact the Dominican Republic native spoke no English, missed his turn on the mound. In fact, he missed the entire game and earned the nickname "I–285," which sympathetic baseball fans familiar with the bypass had embroidered on the back of a Braves warmup jacket and presented to him in pre-game ceremonies later in the season.

"I–285" Perez is no longer with the Atlanta Braves, and the last account anyone had of his whereabouts was that he was on the monster somewhere in the vicinity of Marietta. Residents there say he drives by about every hour-and-a-half, with some handing food and drink to him as he passes.

You will also feel right at home with the Atlanta restaurants and the menus they offer. Such delicacies as quiche, chicken teriyaki, beef stroganoff, tuna Rockefeller, guacamole, spanakopita, shrimp scampi, chicken cacciatore, rice pilaf, vitello tonnato, moo goo gai pan, paella de Manhattan, oysters Rockefeller, chicken Kiev, and pasta have long since replaced such Southern standards as fried chicken, pork chops, chicken and dumplings, tripe, country ham, pickled pig's feet, chitterlings (chitlins), streak-o-lean, mullet, and grits. And waiters with cute names like Keith, Ralph, Pierre, Jordan, and Kirk have replaced such "How y'all" waitresses with born-again names like Mary Nell, Robbie Sue, Johnnie Faye, Emmy Lou, Ellie Mae, and Lawsy Me. Plus, most Atlanta restaurants now accept credit cards and take reservations—two real dyed-in-the-wool innovations.

The language? Don't sweat it. You could possibly go for months and never hear a southern accent, unless you make an appointment with one of the many "Suthen spoke by 'pointment" parlors where young ladies of the South will recite selected portions of *Gone with the Wind* and *Tobacco Road* for "a nominal fee, Honey Chile."

There you have it. If you're from "up yonder" and are moving to Atlanta, disregard what's coming next. But if by chance you have seen the light and plan to migrate further down south to roost forever more, take heed.

By keeping the following do's and don'ts in mind, you will enhance the quality of life once you've settled into your own place in heaven—Dixie:

Do

• Learn to say "Howdy" as soon as possible after re-locating. "Hoi" just won't get the message across, and there are some who will think you are making reference to some Chinese political leader.

• Buy a shotgun, even if you can't shoot it and never load it. It's status in Dixie, bottom line status.

• Purchase some make of pickup truck with a gun rack in the back window and hang the shotgun there. Not only will it complete the picture of a previously bar-ren back window but will also brand you in most cir-cles as "O.K."

• Hide all your bowling trophies. One deer head mounted on the wall in your den will overshadow all your bowling trophies. There are stores available where deer heads can be bought or rented. Besides, you can take pictures of it and send it

back to the boys in the shop. They will be amazed inasmuch as the only deer they ever saw was probably in "Wild Kingdom."

• Learn to stick a little snuff in your cheek, and maybe a wad of Levi Garrett now and again. The first week or two your wife will have to launder your shirts a lot, but once you get the hang of spitting you'll be able to clear a parking meter or drown a fly from six paces. You can easily learn to spit by observing the natives, and should you progress to the point where you are able to dip snuff or chew tobacco and eat boiled peanuts at the same time, you qualify to give lessons. But remember, *always* spit downwind.

• Learn to eat boiled peanuts. Eating chitlins is not a prerequisite to acceptance in the South, contrary to what you may have heard. Boiled peanuts are a staple; chitlins are not. Most men of the South have never tasted one and never will. It is the one thing that, when being cooked, will cause the flies to make every effort to get *out* of the house. I heard it said that some years ago a man in deep South Georgia

dropped one on the kitchen floor, and his cat spent the better part of an hour trying to cover it up.

• Give all your knickers to the Salvation Army before moving South. Also your plaid and argyle socks that go along with them. While they might have been "the things" to wear on the links at prestigious and exclusive golf courses in Westchester and Ann Arbor, they are as out of place in Waycross and Alma as would be the Grand Dragon of the Ku Klux Klan at an NAACP convention.

• Remove all the polish from your nails before leaving for God's country. It just wouldn't look right for a fella' to be frog gigging, skinning rabbits, and cleaning catfish with manicured nails.

• Learn to change the oil in your car, put a new tailpipe and muffler on a pickup, and fix a stopped-up drainpipe. Dixie men pride themselves on being able to fix things for themselves, and the ones who aren't adept at such things have wives who are. Heck, there are ten-year-old girls in the South who can overhaul a tractor, lay brick, and butcher a cow with the best of 'em.

- Learn to play poker if you don't already know how. This alone will ensure that you receive many invitations to fish camps, deer hunting camp houses, and oceanfront condos owned by the local doctors and shifty bootleggers. I know many men who go to fish camps, deer hunting camp houses, and oceanfront condos with regularity and never take a fishing pole, deer rifle, or bathing suit with them. But then, thanks to enterprising shopkeepers, there are adequate establishments and roadside stands where a mess of fish, a deer head, and a tanning parlor suntan can be purchased—credit cards accepted, even for Bicycle and Ace playing cards.

- Invest in a bass boat and park it where it can be easily seen in your yard. And join the local sportsmen's club. The boat will provide visible evidence that you are a good ole boy, and membership in the sportsmen's club will assure you of hearing the best and most current lies.

- Come up with a nickname before or soon after your arrival. Initials are acceptable. *Buster* and *Bubba* are used with such regularity that I suggest you try others on for size, you know, one that fits your personality. *Buddy* and *Slick* are popular, but neither is presently in use to the point of saturation. So are *Dude* and *Cuz*. There are people in my hometown who've known each other for more than forty years and still don't know each other's name. They go with nicknames. *Sloppy* is another one that has some character to it, but then I don't know how you dress or eat. Bear in mind that a nickname says an awful lot about a feller.

- Find yourself a morning coffee group and apply for membership. After all, how else are you going to know what's going on in Washington and Moscow? The coffee table is where you get the straight skinny, right from the horse's mouth as we say in the South. It will help if you are a veteran because most coffee tables fight the wars every morning, primarily World War II and Vietnam. Nothing has changed. We're still the winner in World War II, and nobody's real sure how Vietnam came out yet.

- Buy a pocket knife if you don't already have one. I'm not talking about a penknife for trimming the cuticle, opening letters, or cutting errant threads from a well-worn coat sleeve or a sweater damaged by your runaway cat. I'm talking about a knife that will clean a fish, sharpen a pencil, neuter a boar hog, or slit a deer's throat. A knife is as much standard equipment in the South as jumper cables.

Do not

• Order Cream of Wheat in any cafe south of Macon.

• Order hot tea at Mel's Juke, located about a six-pack north of Broxton and two Willie Nelson tapes south of Macon.

• Turn down an invitation from your new neighbor to go coon hunting with him. The very fact that he invited you is one of the highest compliments you could receive; it means you've been accepted.

• Accept the offer from any owner of a pecan stand to roll the dice or draw high card to see if you pay double or nothing for the bag of pecans you purchased. A few years back a steel worker from Pittsburgh took the bait, and when the con artist finished with him he had been divested of his money orders, two diamond rings, a gold bracelet, and his wife's pearls. The word drifted back that the poor guy ended up going to a Christmas party back home wearing a seersucker suit and perforated shoes. Plus the fact he had to hitchike to the party.

• Go snipe hunting with the boys unless you are prepared to spend the night alone in an isolated ditch far removed from civilization.

• Partake of any liquid that is clear as water that is stored in a gallon jug or quart jar. While it appears harmless, novice sippers of the white stuff have been known to do strange things after partaking, like the retired banker from Buffalo who overindulged, climbed the town water tank and proceeded to remove all his clothes and bark at an imaginary moon. He eventually descended from his lofty perch and ran through town buck naked, stopping only momentarily when he found himself the center of attraction at the monthly meeting of the local garden club before continuing to sprint to

his home. His fiasco wasn't a complete disaster, however, as he was notified later that he had won first prize for "best dried arrangement."

• Shoot pool with any man who asks, "Wanna' shoot f'r five dollars? I ain't very good at it but I like to shoot." There is a good possibility that he is the town hustler who has sent two kids to college and bought a small farm with his winnings over the past five years.

• Put sugar on your grits or make an attempt to eat fried chicken or fish with a knife and fork.

• Ask the sheriff for directions to the union hall or wear your pinky ring in public. The absence of unions is the primary reason so much industry has moved in, and pinky rings flat won't get it in Dixie. In fact, legend has it that a New Yorker holed up in a small South Georgia town back in the late 1940s and began trying to sell pinky rings from the trunk of his Buick, only to be run out of town in less than 48 hours by the local sheriff and two burly deputies, both veterans of the Big War. "You in patrotick country heah, boy. We ain't got no room for Commonists," the sheriff told him.

• Order anything to eat that has a name with foreign

connotations. Chances are your neighbors are convinced that no food item forced to go through immigration can compare favorably with the "grown down home variety."

• Eat collards or liver just to try and impress the natives. A vast majority would touch neither with a galvanized tongue and a cast iron stomach, and will talk about you if you do.

• Play poker with any man named "Doc" or eat in any establishment named "Mom's."

• Flash your credit cards around indiscriminately. They are gradually catching on in the rural South, but cold hard cash is still the way go to for now.

• Ask any woman at the church supper if her pie is a frozen one. This is the ultimate insult to southern women, and you might well end up wearing the pie instead of eating it. They're dead serious about their cooking.

• Ask for milk or bread by those designations only. You should specify "sweet" milk and "white" bread. And never ask for pumpernickel. Waitresses and cafe owners don't cotton to being insulted.

• Propose to a woman unless you're dead serious. They are, and so are their big ole mean Daddies. And remember this: In many areas of Dixie a formal wedding is one at which the father of the bride carries a white shotgun.

• Ever fail to stand when "Dixie" is played. Southerners are just as serious about "Dixie" as Daddies are about proposals to their daughters.

• Play poker or shoot craps with any man who wears long sleeves. It will greatly increase your chances of at least breaking even.

• Walk on the sidewalk without keeping your head down. Not only is tobacco juice nasty, it's also very slippery. What could be worse than for your friends in Yankeeland to read in the local tabloid that your demise came as result of a broken neck from having slipped in a puddle of tobacco juice? Ice and snow they might understand. Tobacco juice? I doubt it.

• Curb your dog in a neighbor's yard. While he probably won't say anything to you about it, just remember that most folks in the South have cows. And wouldn't that make for an interesting obituary back home? Ice and snow they might understand. Cow dung? I doubt it.

• Take it for granted that just because an oncoming car is signaling for a left turn with his turn signal that he will actually make one. Somehow, it just doesn't always work out that way in the Southland.

• Act surprised if everyone you meet on the street signals a greeting to you, even though you don't know the sender of said greeting. Even drivers do this by lifting the right forefinger off the steering wheel and waving it back and forth. I realize that natives of Detroit, Chicago, New York, Philadelphia, and Newark do this also, but the big difference is that they use a different finger.

• Decline an invitation to visit a neighbor's garden. It is probably his pride and joy, and the main reason he has one is so he can raise delicious fresh vegetables—and then give them away.

• Ask a southern girl under the age of fourteen for a date, unless you are absolutely certain that her divorce is final.

WHEN RELOCATING—BONE UP ON THE BASICS

Believe me, it would be an absolute disaster for virgin travelers or transplants to go South without at least making some basic preparations. Nothing he's experienced in life will have prepared the unsuspecting Yankee for what he or she is about to experience.

I have some suggestions that should help in making the adjustment easier and could spare untold embarrassment. And bear in mind that the helpful suggestions offered here are only the basics.

SUGGESTIONS FOR YANKEES MOVING SOUTH:

- Don't, I repeat, *don't* make any attempt to learn to say "How y'all" with the idea that it will make acceptance in the South easier. Forget it! A true Rebel can detect a counterfeit "How y'all" as quick as he can a "How's y'r mommer 'n 'em?"

- If your plan is to become a permanent resident of Dixie, at least get on a first name basis with such country music legends as Willie Nelson, Randy Travis, Roy Acuff, Ricky Skaggs, Loretta Lynn, "Alabama," Barbara Mandrell, and Little Jimmy Dickens. Invest in a few cassette tapes and listen to them while commuting to and from work every day. And it would help if you knew that the Grand Ole Opry is located in Nashville, Tennessee, and not in North Bergen, New Jersey.

- Practice walking slow.

- Learn to chew tobacco. Get yourself a pack of Levi

Garrett, pop a wad in your mouth, stand on the George Washington Bridge, and practice spitting in the Hudson River. And don't worry about polluting it. Somebody already beat you to it.

• Wear long-sleeve white shirts, but roll the sleeves up as far as you can.

• If you want to go the second mile, try your hand at drinking buttermilk. And contrary to what you might think, I have it on good authority that your insides won't resemble the glass from which you drank the buttermilk when it dries.

• Go ahead and make a small investment in at least two pairs of white socks, one for weekly wear and one for Sunday, weddings, and funerals.

• Do not invest in a pink plastic flamingo for the front yard or a Confederate flag for the den. You will see an ample supply of both at hundreds of roadside stands once you cross the state line into South Carolina.

• Try and wean yourself away from quiche and hot tea before heading South. One is nonexistent in Dixie, and the other is in short supply due to a lack of demand for it.

• Once you hit Georgia, buy some boiled peanuts and a Coca-Cola (Cocoler) and practice eating and

drinking while driving. It is established practice in the Peach State. (Fear not the inability to locate boiled peanuts and a Coca-Cola. Both are readily available in the same type Georgia roadside stands as the ones in South Carolina featuring pink plastic flamingos and Confederate flags.)

• Never make reference in the South to the fact that you would really love to have a bagel. You do, and when you wake up the next morning your yard will be overflowing with cute little hound dogs.

• Go to your local library and read up on cotton, soybeans, peanuts, grits, cornmeal, hushpuppies, cane syrup, dove hunting, bass fishing, barbeque, overalls, collards, and chitterlings (chitlins). A general knowledge of these items will open many doors for you; in the case of chitlins, it will close many.

• You may want to consider dropping your first and middle names and use only the initials. Initials are big down South, and nobody questions what they stand for. They are just accepted.

• A few weeks before actually pulling up and heading south, practice "hanging out" a lot. Find a gas station, a pool room, a coffee shop, or a vacant lot and just stand around. Jingle the change in your pocket, tie and untie a piece of string, make marks and lines in the dirt with the toe of your shoe—then rub them out and repeat, using the heel. While it won't be too good for your shoes, it will say a lot for your lifestyle and will eliminate many questions by others hanging out with you down here.

• It might be well for you to brush up on the stock market. A lot of folks where you'll be moving to are pretty well into it and have been for many years. Now then, when I make reference to the stock market I ain't talkin' 'bout IBM, Xerox, Polaroid, GM, Ford, Texaco, AT&T, or Dow-Jones. I'm talkin' 'bout hogs (number ones and number twos), cows, wheat, corn, soybeans, peanuts, oats, and pork bellies.

ROBBIE NELL BELL—THE HOSTESS WITH THE MOSTEST

If you've traveled to the Southland in recent years, you have no doubt noticed that various states down here have gone all out to ensure that visitors to these hallowed grounds are welcomed with open arms. In fact, there are probably more welcome centers south of the Mason–Dixon Line than there are golf courses, juke joints, and Baptist churches.

You know how it goes at official state-owned welcome centers. Each features a huge parking lot, an information counter in the lobby with a portrait of the governor on the wall alongside the state seal, free maps, his and hers rest rooms, and a sample of the state's most recognizable product. In Florida, it's orange juice. In Georgia, it could be a couple of pecans or a slice of watermelon. During the days of the Jimmy Carter administration, it also included a few pea-

nuts. It's apple cider in North Carolina and possibly a firecracker of a peach in South Carolina. Plus the hostesses are programmed to smile for eight hours—no matter what time they got home the night before—and not to pop their chewing gum. They are also bilingual, speaking both Rebel and Yankee fluently.

This is what a tourist can expect at the official state-owned welcome centers. But there are others—the inland, privately owned welcome centers with their own brand of hostesses who not only pop their gum at will but also stick it behind their ear from time to time. One such establishment is Mel's Juke, located about a six-pack north of Broxton, Georgia, on U.S. 341, where Georgia's most popular hostess, Robbie Nell Bell, from Alma (Robbie Nail Bail, fum Almer), rules the roost and welcomes Rebels and Yankees alike in her capacity as head (and only) waitress.

Mel (last name unknown) opened his juke in 1978, shortly after he was paroled. He took a short course in barbeque cooking from Bobo Barfield, who was paroled four years, seven months, three weeks, and two days prior to Mel's release. (Mel and Bobo just have a way of keeping up with time, having served quite a bit of it.) After learing from Bobo just when to turn the meat, Mel made what has proved to be his best move as a juke joint

Miss South Georgia Redneck

owner: he hired Robbie Nell Bell at age thirteen. She is a loyal and trusted employee, a great waitress, and probably Georgia's best-known unofficial welcome center hostess.

Robbie Nell has come a long way since signing on with Mel. Her reputation is known far and wide, as are her accomplishments. While she may just look like your everyday run-of-the-mill beautiful juke joint waitress, looks can be deceiving. Here are just a few honors and achievements that have come her way in the past five years:

• Named Miss South Georgia Redneck: 1985.
• Georgia State Eight-Ball Champion: 1984, 1985, 1986.
• Middle Georgia Mud-Wrestling Champion: 1984, 1985.
• Named Miss Stock Car Racing (The girl race drivers would rather shift gears with): 1984.
• Unanimous choice for induction into the Female Redneck Hall of Fame, Willacoochee, Georgia: 1986.
• First Place, Big Red's Barbeque Cook-off, Vienna, Georgia: 1987.

Robbie Nell is a favorite of the Yankee tourists who stop

regularly at Mel's on their annual trek to Florida. The girl probably knows more about the ways of Yankees than anybody else in Georgia.

"I ain't never been up nawth, an' I ain't got no plans to go, but I lak my Yankee customers. Oh, they git uppity sometimes an' think they know ever'thing—but tha's awright. They tip good," she says. "But I git even with 'em. Ever time one gives me a quarter to put in the juke, I play country music. Course they ain't nothin' ailse on Mel's jukebox. Mel says if it ain't country he don't want it. Only one he won't 'low on the juke is 'The Green, Green Grass of Home.' Says it brings back sad memories, an' I can understan' that."

At the ripe old age of 23, Robbie Nell has been married three times, has a three-year-old boy, and at present has no plans to walk down the aisle again. Her third marriage, to Urel Simpson, was a disaster. They were married in the reposing room of his uncle's funeral home using leftover flowers and went on their honeymoon in the funeral home hearse. Urel surmised that by doing so he would save the cost of a motel room and also advertise his uncle's funeral home. It got a little embarrassing toward the end of the honeymoon when, while driving up to see Rock City near Chattanooga, Tennessee, the back door flew open and the cot rolled down the mountain. And not only was it embarrassing, it was expensive. Urel had to spring for a motel room that night, but the next day he cut the honeymoon short and drove back home, only to be arrested upon his return for leaving the state without permission, thereby violating the terms of his probation.

The divorce followed, and at last report Urel was operating a worm ranch and cricket farm south of Waycross and going steady with a woman wrestler from Jacksonville.

Robbie Nell? She's holding down the fort and ruling the roost at Mel's. Footloose and fancy free, she's practicing every day to defend her championship in the upcoming Georgia State Eight-Ball Tournament in Jesup. Robbie Nell's probably the best thing to happen to tourism in the South since the advent of the interstate highway system and radar detectors.

A TRIPLE DOSE OF HUSBAND

I thought I probably should explain more about Robbie Nell's wedding to Urel Simpson, so I took a look at some old notes I made just before the big event. Here—in only slightly edited form—is a behind-the-scenes look at the happy event.

On a trip to Waycross, I stopped off at Mel's Juke, about a six-pack north of Broxton, for a barbecue sandwich. Mel broke the news—of Robbie Nail's impending wedding.

"Where's Robbie Nail?"

"Still up north," Mel said. "She's gonna' git married again in July," Mel said. "Marryin' a good ole boy fum over Douglas way. Name's Urel Simpson (properly pronounced 'You-rail Seeumpson'). Kinda' nice that their names rhyme, ain't it? Y'know, Robbie Nail and You-rail?"

"Yeah, nice," I agreed. "Where's the weddin' gonna' be, Mel?"

"In the reposin' room at Seeumpson's Funeral Home, where You-rail works in the daytime," Mel said.

"Where You-rail works in the daytime? What about at night? Does he work at night?" I asked.

"Tha's a big ten-four."

"Where? Where does he work at night?"

"Well, he don't talk 'bout that," Mel said.

"Oh, I see. Has You-rail been married before?"

"Yeah, once't. Right in that same reposin' room, too. Married a woman truck driver from over Savannah way. I was bes' man, an' like his daddy said after th' weddin', 'he shore looked natural.'"

"I'll bet he did. Will there be a reception after the wedding, Mel?"

"Doggone right! Havin' it rat cheer like we've always done whenever Robbie Nail got married," Mel said with pride.

"You got enough room? Looks a little small to me."

"Got plenty o' room. You-rail's borrowin' a tent from the funeral home to set up out by th' barbecue pit. An' cheers, too. His uncle, what owns the funeral home, tol' him he could have all th' cheers he needed, provided of course they won't no funeral that day," Mel allowed. "Ya' want 'nother samich?"

"No thanks. One's just enough. Good, too," I told him. "Say, Mel, you heard from Robbie Nail lately?"

"Kinda' second-hand, I have. She called my mama fum Nashville las' week to talk about th' weddin' an th' reception. You know, woman talk," he said.

"Yeah, like what to serve, how many people to invite, and all that," I suggested.

"Right, an' th' honeymoon," Mel said, "Can't fergit th' honeymoon."

"Where are they goin'?"

"Well, I kinda' figger they'll go to Jaykull. Robbie Nail always goes to Jaykull on her honeymoons. 'Course, now if'n they's a funeral the day o' th' weddin' they ain't goin' nowhere 'cept to th' Shady Oaks Motel over on Highway 86," Mel allowed.

"Why not? What's a funeral got to do with Robbie Nail and You-rail's honeymoon?"

"It's got ever'thing to do with it," Mel said. "You-rail ain't got no car so he's plannin' on usin' th' hearse to take Robbie Nail to Jaykull."

"No car? Where's his car?" I asked.

"Ain't got one. Has somethin' to do with his night work," Mel said. "Th' GBI caught him down close to Blackshear and took it. Gonna' be sold at a auction next month. Dang good car, too. A '81 Trans-Am, with overdrive an' ever'thing. I rode with him fum Douglas to Tifton 'bout six months ago an' that sucker'll straight fly!"

"So, everything is all set? For the reception, I mean."

"Yeah, Mama's headin' th' food an' I'm handlin' th' drinks," Mel said.

"You planning on serving things like caviar, herring, and anchovies?"

"Naw, I ain't servin' no wine. Jus' longneck Bud an' Colt 45, with some Meller Yeller f'r th' young'uns," Mel said.

Is Robbie Nail for real? You bet your pickup she's for real—and so's Mel, who runs his juke joint about a six-pack north of Broxton.

IS THERE NO CULTURE IN THE SOUTH?

It happened to me again last week, at a cocktail party. I was backed into a corner by a pair of New Jersey American transplants, now enjoying the good life in Middle Georgia after serving a near-life sentence in the Garden State.

The whole thing started after I sat down at what I thought was an unoccupied table, bent on enjoying a cup of coffee. No way.

I had no more than sipped when they appeared at the table, took their seats, and introduced themselves. It seems that they were there before me but left to go wherever Yankee transplants go when they up and leave their table at a cocktail party.

Following the introductions, we engaged in the usual chatter that goes on at cocktail parties—the state of the weather, the state of the nation, high prices, the quality of the hors d'oeuvres, and family backgrounds—to establish the proper pedigree, you know.

I learned, among other things, that they migrated south from New Jersey after retirement. No surprise. I mean, after all, have you ever heard of anyone retiring to the North?

And they learned that I'd spent a few years in New Jersey, 1960–67, an eternity for a Georgia boy.

The conversation was rocking along smoothly until the female rubbed salt in my redneck wound with this observation: "I enjoy living down here in the South, except for one thing," she said, baiting me.

I took the bait and asked, "Yes? And what's that?"

"No culture. I miss the culture that I enjoyed in New Jersey and New York," she said.

I gritted my teeth real hard, gulped down what was left of my coffee, and counted to ten. I'd been in this corner before and really had no intention of making a scene. Finally, I asked her, "And what culture is it that you enjoyed up there that you miss so much down here?"

"Oh, things like the theater, art galleries, museums, excellent restaurants," she said. "Always something to do. But down here, nothing. Don't you find that to be true?"

"No, not really," I said. "It was my observation that of the eight million people in New York, about all 98 percent of them did was talk about the culture—the theatre, and such—but they never went."

"Well, at least it was there if you wanted it," she said.

I just had to ask the next question, and did.

"By the way, what prompted you two to move to Georgia? Do you have relatives here?"

"Oh, no. I just told Frank that the day he retired from his job in Brooklyn we were moving south, to either Flor-

ida or Georgia," she said. "We looked at Florida and decided on Georgia, Middle Georgia."

"A wise choice," I said, "but why leave all that culture in New York?"

"Well, the last year we lived up there we were robbed twice and mugged once," she said. "That did it. I decided to get out."

While establishing our individual pedigrees, I learned that they had lived in Oradell, New Jersey. I recalled that Oradell was also the hometown of one of our astronauts, Walter Shirra, who went into space in 1962. (I was living there at the time and would gladly have gone with him to get out of New Jersey.)

"Yes, we're very proud of Wally Shirra," said the husband.

"And understandably so,"

I said. "But he sure picked a heck of a way to get out of New Jersey, didn't he?"

"How's that?" the man asked.

"Took a space ship, Mercury 8. Talk about desperate," I said.

The female sipped her coffee, raised her painted eyebrows, and said, "Well, I still miss the culture in New York."

"Yeah, I reckon so. But you don't miss them robbers and muggers a whole helluva' lot, do you, ma'am?" I asked.

"Well, let me put it this way, we're not planning to move back," she said.

I thought about 'em all the way home. I'm gonna have to invite 'em to a cane grindin' or a peanut boilin', I reckon. It's a shame they're not takin' advantage of what culture we do have here, right?

SECTION FOUR

WHAT'S TO EAT?

YANKEE DINING CAN BE AN ETHNIC NIGHTMARE

Until I ventured north to live in Detroit in 1955, the word *ethnic* was a stranger to me. I had never heard of it. Ethnic neighborhood? In the small southern towns where I was raised, you simply lived on one side of town or the other—with the haves or the have-nots. This is not so in Detroit. The folks who live there live and breathe ethnically, in their own neighborhoods.

What it means is that those with common backgrounds live and shop in their own neighborhood, attend their own churches, and speak their own language. And they eat their own native foods. You have the Polish in Hamtramck, the Italians in Grosse Pointe, The Greeks in East Detroit, and the Southerners spread out along East Jefferson in the neighborhood of the Chrysler plant. It took me a while to find it out, but a fella' can go in a restaurant out near the Chrysler plant, order grits, streak-o-lean, cornbread, and buttermilk, and get it without everybody in the establishment looking at you like you just escaped or something. And you can get "sirrup" for your biscuits instead of "seerup."

Always bear this in mind when eating out in any eating establishment north of Knoxville: If you order "sirrup" and the waitress asks, "What kind, cane or maple?" you're in big trouble. You're in double trouble if she pronounces the delicacy "seerup." A good rule of thumb is to remember that "sirrup" is intended by the good Lord to be sopped. He was good enough to make "seerup" for the faint of heart and quiche eaters of the world.

During my seven-year stint in Detroit, I developed a first name relationship with food that Grandma would never have allowed inside her house. Ethnic food is fine if you happen to be an ethnic, but if you happen to be just a plain Southerner it won't work.

On one occasion I got stuck with something called "chlodnick" (a salt cucumber soup with sour cream) and "flaki populski" (tripe prepared with dumplings, grated cheese and paprika). Not only did I not eat it, I wouldn't dare say it out loud in front of Mama and Daddy.

I also got wrapped up in something in Grosse Pointe that has the unpalatable name of "zabaglione" (made from egg yolks, sugar, Marsala wine, and a few other things that housewives throw away down in South Georgia and North Florida). I was brave enough to try the place again a few months later, however, and ended up face to face with "alla Millinese" (rice cooked in butter with beef marrow and grated cheese). You know how it is. When the Italians ain't real sure, they just dump in a load of grated cheese—like Mama always added water to the grits and kept on adding

vinegar and salt to the collards.

One of my more interesting ethnic dining experiences came at a fine restaurant in the Greektown section of Detroit, the Grecian Gardens. In a Greek restaurant it makes absolutely no difference what you order: it is served with rice. If the place served Vienna sausage or Moon Pies, they would be served on a bed of rice.

It was in the Grecian Gardens that this ole country boy was introduced to "Souvlakia" (tidbits of lamb marinated in oil with onions, tomatoes, and bacon). Naturally, it is served with rice. I also had a generous serving of "Moussaka" (alternate layers of minced lamb, sliced vegetables, potatoes covered with a cheese sauce, and, once again, served on a bed of rice).

I learned one thing from eating in Greek restaurants in Detroit: lamb is a menu biggie. I never got used to eating lamb. Somehow I always associated eating lamb with child molesting—You know, like "Mary had a little lamb"—and I just sort of felt a little guilty about eating it. Maybe if the nursery rhyme had been written "Mary had a little pig (or calf)," I wouldn't be too hiked up about eating pork chops and steak either. But a little lamb?

My initial exposure to pumpernickel bread also came in Detroit. I'll never forget it. The exposure came in a German delicatessen, and I'd never heard of a delicatessen before sliding into Detroit in 1955. The natives call them delis, and they serve strange food, like pumpernickel bread and meats I still can't pronounce.

I went to Kreuger's Deli with a fellow FBI agent, Christopher Kokolakis, a Greek. He ordered a sandwich: corned beef on pumpernickel bread. Not wanting to complicate things, I ordered the same. I had no idea what I was getting because corned beef wasn't a biggie in South Georgia. Pumpernickel? I wouldn't have dared to order such a thing in Holder's Cafe back home, not out loud in mixed company. Mrs. Holder would have told my Mama for sure.

The service was great, and our sandwiches arrived before you could say "Gesundheit!" I stared at mine in disbelief for a full two minutes before figuring out where I'd seen one before: in my Grandpa's pasture back home where it had been run over twice by his tractor and lay in the sun for two weeks in mid-July. I vowed right then and there that I wasn't about to eat no black bread that looked like it had been dropped and stepped on.

The pumpernickel bread wasn't my lone mistake at Kreuger's Deli. I also ordered tea. Up in Detroit when you order tea with no further explanation you get hot tea. The only folks I ever heard of drinking hot tea were sick people and Englishmen. I wasn't sick, and the closest I ever came to England was reading about it in high school.

I didn't want to cause no ruckus with Kreuger, seeing as how he was a big, mean German and all, plus we were only ten years removed from fighting folks like him. So I nibbled on the sandwich and played around with the hot tea as best I could, trying my best not to let either Kokolakis or Kreuger know that I was a rookie pumpernickel eater and hot tea drinker.

I was doing fairly well until Kokolakis suggested that we have dessert and ordered for both of us, probably sens-

ing that I was indeed treading in unfamiliar waters. He scanned the menu and finally settled on something called apfelstrudel. While it sounded subversive to me, I raised no objection and played around with it for a few minutes, but that was it. I wouldn't put that stuff on a wart, much less in my mouth.

I finally left Kreuger's Deli completely amazed at what ethnic food really was, or how all the ethnicans learned to pronounce it.

Later in the day I went to Shorty's Lunch out near the Chrysler plant and ate some backbone and rice, three vegetables, cornbread, banana pudding, and iced tea. And I burped real loud and long when I got back in my car.

DINING IN A MAFIA DEN

Funny thing, but I always feel like I'm reading a list of witnesses scheduled to testify before the Senate Sub-Committee on Racketeering when I read a menu in an Italian restaurant. And even worse, I see all the witnesses seated around the restaurant. How would you feel if you were surrounded by the pro bowlers of the underworld and made your living as an FBI agent? It happened to me in an Italian restaurant shortly after transferring to New York in the early 1960s.

It didn't take me long to match up the characters scattered around the dining room with the names on the witness list, including some who weren't even subpoenaed. My Hoover-trained eyes scanned the room cautiously until I had identified each one, along with a girlfriend or two.

Seated back in a dimly lit alcove at a table for four were the two Mafia chieftans and their girlfriends for the evening. I recognized them right away from previously viewed mugshots: "Veal" Scalopini and his doll, "Steak" Diane, along with "Beef" Stroganoff and his long-time mistress, "Quiche" Lorraine. "Veal" and "Beef" were inhaling long black cigars. "Steak" and "Quiche" were likewise inhaling glasses of expensive wine.

At one end of the bar—alone—was the money man of the mob, "Oysters" Rockefeller. He said nothing. With one hand he repeatedly tossed a silver dollar in the air, and with the other he held on tightly to a small black bag. "Oysters" never once looked at the coin he was tossing and never once failed to catch it when it came down. Obviously the result of prolonged practice in this and many other New York bars.

Standing by the cigarette machine, no doubt owned by the mob, was the unmistakable "Eggs" Benedict. His hand rested on top of the machine and melodiously tapped out a tune known but to "Eggs." A cigarette dangled from his lips, and his spit-shine black shoes glistened in the stingy light. Why he wore sunglasses was, and always has been, a mystery.

Far removed from the crowd were the two that I pegged to be the informers, whose days were numbered: "Chicken" Cacciatore and "Shrimp" Scampi. They were seated at a table near the men's room, munching pistachio nuts and sipping imported beer. Both "Chicken" and "Shrimp" were visibly nervous, and rightfully so. Both were destined to be kissed on the cheek before the sun rose again. All informers eventually get kissed by the mob.

In due time "Beef" gave a slight nod of his head and all his compatriots, with the exception of "Chicken" and "Shrimp," adjourned to a back room. The Senate Committee would have to wait. Mafia court was in session, and the jury would determine the fate of the two informers.

"Steak" and "Quiche?" They could care less. Just keep the wine coming. . . .

DIETING UNDER STRESS
. . . in the North and the South

Sometimes I get the feeling that everybody from "Fatty" Arbuckle to Jack Spratt's wife has come up with some sort of diet. Well, I have yet another one for you. It's called "Dieting Under Stress," and was sent to two friends of mine by their son who lives and works in Atlanta. Near as I can tell, it works equally well for Yankees as Southerners. It's called "The Stress Diet." The way I figure, the diet is what causes the stress!

This diet is designed to help you cope with the stress that builds up during the day.

BREAKFAST:
  ½ Grapefruit
  1 Slice Whole Wheat Toast, Dry
  8 oz. Skim Milk
LUNCH:
  4 oz. Lean Broiled Chicken Breast
  1 Cup Steamed Spinach
  1 Cup Herb Tea
  1 Oreo Cookie
MIDAFTERNOON SNACK:
  Rest of the Oreos in the package
  2 Pints Rocky Road Ice Cream
  1 Jar Hot Fudge Sauce
  Nuts, Cherries, Whipped Cream
DINNER:
  2 Loaves Garlic Bread with Cheese
  Large Sausage, Mushroom and Cheese Pizza
  4 Cans or 1 large Pitcher of Beer
  3 Milky Way Candy Bars
LATE EVENING NEWS SNACK:
  Entire Frozen Cheesecake, Eaten Directly from Freezer

RULES FOR THIS DIET

1. If you eat something and no one sees it, it has no calories.

2. If you drink a diet drink with a candy bar, the calories in the candy bar are cancelled out by the diet drink.

3. When you eat with someone else, calories don't count if you don't eat more than they do.

4. Food used for medicinal purposes **never** counts, like hot chocolate, brandy, toast and Sara Lee Cheesecake.

5. If you fatten up everyone else around you, you look thinner.

6. Movie-related foods do not have additional calories because they are part of the entire entertainment package and not part of one's personal fuel, like Milk Duds, buttered popcorn, Hershey Bars (with or without almonds), Junior Mints, Red Hots and Tootsie Rolls.

7. Cookie pieces contain no calories. The process of breaking causes calorie drainage.

8. Things licked off knives and spoons have no calories provided you are in the process of preparing something. Examples are peanut butter on a knife while make a peanut butter and jelly sandwich and ice cream on a spoon while making a sundae.

9. Foods that have the same color have the same number of calories. Examples are spinach and pistachio ice cream, cottage cheese and banana cream pie, mushrooms and white chocolate. (**Note:** Chocolate is a universal color and may be substituted for any other food color.)

10. For every burp, subtract 25 calories.

TURKEY RECIPES COOKED HIS GOOSE

On a recent trip to Washington, D.C., I ran into an acquaintance I hadn't seen for several years. Since I last saw him, his status in Washington society had deteriorated, which reminded me of how uncertain life there can be.

People there ebb and flow like the tide, and shift up and down like the stock market. One day a fella' can be in the penthouse enjoying quiche and rare wine, while the next he might well be occupying the outhouse slurping dishwater soup and stale coffee dipped and poured by some agency with a government grant in a makeshift shelter within a stone's throw of the White House. Indeed, life can be tough in Washington.

The last time I had talked with him he had been the White House breakfast chef, having been brought to Washington by Jimmy Carter in 1976.

The former chef's name is "Buster" Ferguson. Prior to making the move to Washington in 1977, Buster was a short order cook at "Granny's House of Grits" located between Plains and Americus, Georgia. In the 50s and 60s Jimmy, Rosalynn, Billy, Miss Lillian and all the Carters were breakfast regulars at Granny's, so it followed that when Jimmy loaded his pickup and headed for Washington he invited Buster to come along in the prestigious role of White House breakfast chef.

"Things rolled along purty good fer awhile," Buster told me as he pulled his coat collar even higher to ward off the Washington wind. "I even had me an official chef's name—Pilaf. Rosalynn give it to me. Said she didn't cotton to nobody named Buster whuppin' up breakfast in the White House kitchen."

"What happened," I asked.

"Seems to me like you had it made, Buster . . . uh, Pilaf."

"Jus' call me Buster," he said with a trace of sorrow and regret in his watery eyes. "Ain't no Pilaf no more."

"Why? Did the Reagan folks kick you out?"

"Oh no, Rosalynn did. Nancy Reagan hired me back las' year."

"Tell me more," I pleaded.

"Well, what happened was this: Jus' before th' 'lection in '80, Rosalynn invited all o' Jimmy's supporters to the White House for breakfas'. She chose the menu—grits an' chitlins. An' I can tell you, Hoss, that breakfas' is whut done me in."

"You mean you got fired?"

"On the spot, soon as th' breakfast was over. Rosalynn tol' Jimmy th' breakfas' was a disaster, an' he agreed. I had my pink slip fo' nine o'clock. She even made me turn in my monnergrammed chef's hat an' apron."

"On what grounds were you fired? I know you are a grits and chitlins expert and. . . ."

"The pink slip was short an' to th' point. All it said was 'You are hearby terminated as of this moment as the White House Breakfast chef.' That was it."

"No reason given?"

"Oh, yeah. In the space where it said 'Reason for Termination' she just gave two reasons."

"And what were they?"

"Lumpy grits an' chewy chitlins!"

"But you say Nancy Reagan hired you back last year. What are you doing out here in the cold in a Salvation Army overcoat and worn-out sneakers?"

"Well, it happened las' week, two days fo' Thanksgiving. Mrs. Reagan gave me my pink slip just before she and Ronnie flew to their California ranch for the holidays. She had asked me to help the dinner crew come up with an unusual turkey dinner this year, and we tried. We tried hard. Hell, she fired us all!"

"All of you?"

"That's a big 10–4," Buster said. "We tried ever'thing in the Washington recipe book but nothin' worked.

"What did you try?"

"We worked on 12 turkey recipes for six days, but none of 'em worked. Wanna' hear 'em?"

"By all means."

Here are the twelve turkey recipes Buster told me they tried, the first three originating with Macon radio station WAYS's morning funny man,

Bill Elder:

1. *Robert Bork Turkey.* It really turned out to be cooked goose, with two right wings.

2. *Joe Biden Turkey.* We found out quick that Biden ain't nothin' more'n a chicken who wants to sound like a turkey.

3. *Dan Rather Turkey.* The problem with Rather turkey is that jus' when you get ready to eat him, he gets up and leaves the table for six minutes.

4. *David Ginsburg Turkey.* We really had a problem with this because the turkey insisted on bringing his own pot.

5. *Oliver North Turkey.* Can you believe this? Every time we got ready to cook him, Fawn Hall stuck the recipe in her underdrawers, ran downstairs to North's office, and shredded it.

6. *Jim Bakker Turkey.* Every time we placed him in the oven we received a note from some girl named Jessica in Babylon, New York, demanding a $265,000 ransom.

7. *Robert Byrd Turkey.* Wouldn't work. There's a policy at the White House that nothing can be served that's been dead more'n twelve years.

8. *Oral Roberts Turkey.* We simply couldn't bring ourselves to roast him. He kept gobbling over and over, "See! I Told You So; Lord, I'm Coming Home!"

9. *Tammy Bakker Turkey.* This one really backfired. It took us three days to remove all the makeup and then we found out that the turkey was actually Grandma Moses.

10. *Gary Hart Turkey.* We had to give up. The Hart turkey demanded that he be served on a bed of Rice.

11. *Ted Kennedy Turkey.* We thought we had it made with this one, but had to abort it when we found out it was a Christmas turkey and saw what it was stuffed with.

12. *Sam Nunn Turkey.* This one blew our minds. As hard as we tried, we could never get a commitment from him as to whether he preferred to be baked or roasted.

I guess Buster summed it up pretty well when he told me, "All things considered, I'd druther be standin' out here in th' cold beggin' soup an' coffee than doin' what I had to do for more'n three years—make strawberry jam and mustard sandwiches on a onion roll for Amy."

SECTION FIVE

RELIGION:
NORTH AND SOUTH

MEDITATING MADE EASY

The welcome centers, rest stops, and roadside parks provided for weary tourists on interstate highways are compliments to the individual states. They provide tangible evidence that tourists are welcome and that thought and consideration have been given to their comfort and well being.

What, for goodness sake, could have been more frustrating in the hectic pre-interstate highway years than to load up the wife and kids in New Jersey and head for Florida on vacation, only to search in vain for rest rooms every thirteen miles on barren two-lane rural highways such as U.S. 301, 25, and 17? The woeful cry from the back seat, "Daddy, I've got to go to the baffroom!" every thirteen miles must have been cause enough to drive a man to drink. Thank goodness the welcome centers, rest stops, and roadside parks along the interstates have done much to alleviate the "baffroom" problem. No doubt they have saved many a Daddy from a ten-week stint in an alcohol rehabilitation center.

While the facilities mentioned now serve travelers well, there remains an obvious void—and I have a plan to eliminate it. The void? Secluded and peaceful meditation areas to satisfy certain religious needs of travelers who sometimes spend as many as two or three weeks motoring around the country, north and south. A designated place to pause, pray, and meditate would no doubt serve a meaningful purpose for millions of travelers.

It is my proposal that we get busy in America and provide for just such a place—at designated intervals—for those who feel the need for prayer and medita-

tion. Of course, there is always the problem of separation of church and state, but it seems to me that the world is filled with more than enough guilt-conscious and compassionate philanthropists quite willing to underwrite the construction of such places.

I have suggested that such a plan be implemented in Florida on a trial basis with four locations: two Protestant and two Catholic. The plan would work this way:

The weary Protestant traveler would exit the interstate and pull into a drive-in shelter, the occupants of the vehicle never having to leave the confines of their automobile to experience the serenity of prayer and meditation. Just pull in, deposit two quarters in the designated slot at the entrance, and prerecorded soft organ music, featuring standard hymns, would play for four minutes. This would allow enough time for the kids to go the "baffroom" and for Mama to powder her nose.

The music is followed by a three-minute period of silence for individual meditation, the lights inside the shelter fading automatically for atmosphere.

At the end of the three minutes, a green light comes

on over the altar, signaling that the session has ended. The driver then proceeds to exit the shelter—much like an automatic car wash—so that one leaves with the feeling that he has "washed his sins away," so to speak.

The Protestant oases I would name simply "Park and Pray."

In providing for the needs of the traveling Catholic, my plan calls for a similar shelter, with one addition: a drive-in 24-hour confessional in which three priests take turns working eight-hour shifts. The driver simply sounds his horn, and the priest on duty welcomes him through an intercom system, very similar to the ones used on visiting day at Sing Sing Prison for relatives and friends to converse with inmates.

The priest hears the confession of the repenter and affords him an opportunity to place something in "the collection plate," an in-and-out drawer, power operated, similar to those employed by banks at drive-in windows.

While I haven't yet concluded what would be an appropriate name for the Catholic oases, I am leaning heavily toward "Toot N' Tell."

A fellow never knows when he might need to avail himself of the services of a priest. You know how the conscience works. A feeling of guilt can strike almost without warning, like the carpenter in Buffalo, New York.

It seems that the little carpenter had for years been stealing lumber from a Buffalo lumberyard. He had stacks and stacks of it stored behind his house. But one day—almost without warning—his conscience got to him and he sought the services of a priest to whom he confessed his long-standing practice of stealing lumber. The priest didn't say anything right away, but finally addressed a question to the little carpenter:

"Do you think you can make a novena?"

"Father," said the little carpenter, "if you've got the plans I've got the lumber!"

STANDIN' IN TH' NEED O' PRAYER

It has been my observation that in times of adversity we all have a tendency to turn to prayer when all else has failed. It is the universal shoulder upon which we cry. There are Protestant prayers and there are Catholic prayers, both employed in times of both need and greed. Here are two prime examples. First, a Protestant prayer.

Many years ago there was a prolonged drought in South Georgia, and people there were near panic. It hadn't rained for months on end and finally a prayer meeting was called to pray for rain. Everyone in attendance was shocked and amazed to see Uncle Jake Barlowe ease inside the little country church and take a seat in back. Jake Barlowe, owner of a very large farm, hadn't been inside a church in more than forty years.

The prayer service went on for more than two hours, and after most had offered up their prayers for rain, Uncle Jake, with the aid of his walking stick, arose slowly from his seat and ambled ever so slowly to the front of the church and slowly knelt at the altar rail. With the church in deafening silence, he cleared his throat loudly and began to pray . . .

"Oh, Lord, this here's Jake Barlowe talkin' an' I come now to ask you to send us a rain. Now then, I ain't talkin' 'bout no shower, you heah? I'm talkin' 'bout a real rain.

"I want a rain that'll make the river banks run over, that'll make roads look like creeks and the ditches turn and churn like they was full of moccasins! We need a rain, Lord, an' to tell you the truth I really don't care if you send one that'll wash away the outhouse an' make 15-inch trenches all over the yard!

"We ain't talkin' here tonight 'bout no shower or no drizzle. No, sir! We want to go outside the house an' watch the lightnin' rip across't the sky in hot blue forks as fat black clouds roll in on us. An' I want us to have to hurry an' close up the house, Lord, with the first fat drops the size of marbles chasin' us an' plunkin' on the hood of the car like pecans fallin' from the tree.

"We want to scramble all over the house, jus' as the first few sheets fall in a sudden risin' wind, frantically slammin' down all the winders while all the chillun' stan' back scared, really scared, with their eyes big as saucers, Lord.

"Oh, Lord of hosts, we want to look out the winders an' watch regiments of close-packed raindrops close ranks an' march diagonally down. We want to hear the gurgle of gutters under the eaves, an' then the sputter of the downspout, an' see a stream o' water shootin' out into the yard more'n eight feet—an' swirlin' round and round in big circles.

"Oh God of Israel, Isaac, and Jacob, let the rain come down so hard, and the drops dance so high, that the streets seem covered with a six-inch deep fog of spatterdrops an' cars an' trucks have to pull over to the side an' wait.

"Then, let it jus' keep up for a while, an' then sorta' begin to taper off gradual like, but then let it turn right aroun' an' get a lot worse— swishin', poundin', slammin', soakin', spatterin', and drenchin', with the thunder comin' 'crackety-bam!' An' the lightnin' flashin' an' streakin' so fast that a feller really can't tell which flash goes with which boom o' thunder; so that all the women folks get scared an' climb on the beds an' scream at the little chillun' not to get too close to the winder. An' the dogs will run under the shed, the cats will scat an' dash to get behind the kitchen stove, an' the chickens will climb to the highes' roost.

"An' then, oh jealous God, repeat the whole shebang 'bout three or four more times so that we'll have to climb up the attic ladder an' put a wash tub under that li'l ole leak in the tin roof that ain't really even hardly noticeable durin' a plain ol' ordinary rain.

"Then, if it be thy will, Lord, after maybe a couple o' hours, kinda' taper it down just a tad, but slow an' easy like. Then, after we're all in bed, keep it up with a business-like rain that comes down real steady til' 'bout good daylight, an' then spits a few more drops from a dark gray sky, coupled with a little goodbye thunder from way off.

"Finally, to tell it like it is, Lord, I want you to send us a rain that'll grow corn—ears of corn as long as my arm, 'cause if they's anything in this world I hate to do it's shuck a damn nubbin! Amen, an' I thank you."

So much for the Protestants. Let us move on to the Catholics:

I think there is nothing quite as pitiful as somebody who really needs to pray but doesn't know how, and there are such people as evidenced in this little story.

During World War II, three soldiers found themselves sharing a foxhole in Normandy during a heavy mortar bombardment. They huddled closely as the mortar shells came closer and closer to their position. One shell exploded so close to them that it appeared certain that the next one would demolish them. Their options had decreased to the point of nothing and none. One of the three suggested that they have prayer, but admitted that he didn't know a prayer or how to pray. He suggested that one of the others offer up a prayer.

"I don't know one, and ain't never prayed," said one.

"Neither do I," said the other.

"But we can't just sit here and do nothing," said the first one.

"Don't either of you know anything religious we can use?"

"Well, when my family lived in New Jersey we lived for a while next door to a Catholic church, and I remember what I heard coming from inside the church once in a while. That's all I know," said one of the other two.

"For goodness sakes, let's use that! We do need to pray, and quick!" said the third. "Will you repeat what you heard?"

"Uh, yeah. I can do that," he replied.

All three bowed their heads and closed their eyes. The mortar shells were exploding all around them. Finally, during a break in the shelling, the former New Jersey resident began. . . .

"Under the B–10. . . ."

A SOUTH GEORGIA METHODIST VISITS ST. PATRICK'S CATHEDRAL

I hadn't been in New York since moving back to Georgia from there in 1965, but in March, 1978, I got the urge to return. I drove to Atlanta, boarded an airplane at 5:30 P.M., and in just over an hour I stepped off at LaGuardia Airport. It was Thursday, March 16. I wanted to spend St. Patrick's Day in the big city, see a Broadway play, and, above all, attend Mass at St. Patrick's Cathedral.

The play, Wiz, was outstanding in the eyes of this amateur critic, but St. Patrick's was unforgettable. There was a special significance in worshiping there on St. Patrick's Day, March 17.

I paused momentarily at the door before entering to survey the setting of this legendary monument to Christianity. To my right, as I stood on the steps before the gigantic bronze doors, was yet another monument, this one to the fashion world— Sak's Fifth Avenue. To my

left was Radio City Music Hall. Across the street, a bar loomed.

I looked upward, as do all tourists in New York, and gazed at the 330-foot spire pointing majestically toward heaven. Before entering St. Patrick's, I glanced back over my shoulder and took another look at the bar across the street.

Once inside, the bronze doors closed behind me and I was, literally, in another world. The rushing, buzzing, scurrying mass of humanity on Fifth Avenue that moments before had surrounded me was no longer in evidence. Though just thirty feet away, it was silent to those of us inside the cathedral.

I couldn't help but smile as I surveyed the spectacle that filled my eyes. St. Patrick's was outdrawing the bar across the street 500 to 1. I hoped God noticed it, too.

I treated myself to the

beauty of the interior and greedily drank it in, becoming intoxicated only on the beauty and serenity of it all. I wished my Daddy could have been at my side, and although dead since 1969, maybe he was. He would have been pleased at the cathedral-bar ratio.

I seated myself near the rear and waited with more than 2,500 others for Mass to begin. I watched others enter and kneel. There was a man, impeccably dressed in a Chesterfield topcoat. He could easily have been chairman of the board at Chase Manhattan Bank, and might have been. He was followed by a battered, wrinkled, and generally unkempt woman wearing a ragged, faded blue sweater. She could easily have been the charwoman who scrubbed the floors at Chase Manhattan, and might have been. It made no difference. When the bronze doors closed behind them, the man and woman immediately became equals—at least for the next hour on earth and for always in the sight of God.

I watched them later, seated side by side, as the offering baskets were passed. I watched them drop their offerings in the basket, smiled, and contemplated a familiar passage of Scripture, "The rich young ruler . . . . the widow's mite."

I was surrounded by candles, burning steadily. I wanted them to talk and tell me the hopes, the prayers, the fears that prompted them to be lit in the first place. Then my eyes moved to the right front pew, the pew that held the Kennedy family for all the world to see on television when Robert F. Kennedy made his final appearance on this earth. An assassin's bullet had ensured that.

I listened intently as Father Charles Mahoney, perched high above the congregation and directly in front of the Kennedy pew, delivered his short sermon. It was impressive and satisfying to the soul. I was proud to be a Christian and part of it all.

When Father Mahoney finished his sermon, I watched as the hundreds strolled forward to the altar to receive Holy Communion. The "banker" and the "charwoman" walked down the long aisle together—and back—as equals.

It was beautiful.

SECTION SIX:

LIFESTYLES IN
THESE DIXIE PLACES

WE DO IT A LITTLE SLOWER IN THE SOUTH

I'll be the first to admit that those of us in the South are pretty much laid back, like if it don't get done today—maybe tomorrow. And if it don't get done tomorrow—to hell with it.

"The road to hell is paved with good intentions." I've heard that all my life, but its true meaning didn't really come home to roost until I was returning home from a trip to Florida. It was almost dark when I pulled into a driveway at a house just south of Callahan, Florida, on U.S. Highway 1, to ask directions.

The house had a porch and a swing, along with a rocking chair. The man I presumed to be the head of the house occupied the swing, and the woman I presumed to be his wife was rocking back and forth in the rocker. Had Norman Rockwell painted a picture of what I saw, he would have drawn in a hound dog stretched out underneath the big oak tree in the yard and a few cats and kittens on one end of the porch.

Had I chosen a name for the man of the house, I couldn't have made a more fitting selection than did his Mama and Daddy years ago. His name is Silas. And I learned that his wife is Nellie, also appropriate for the rural setting.

I got out of my car, approached, the front steps, and called out the customary greeting, "Howdy!"

"Howdy," Silas said in return. "Come on in."

I continued walking toward the steps and upon reaching them, stepped on the lower one—not in the middle mind you, but on one end. The step was not nailed down and the other end shot up like a jumping board. I caught myself with both hands as I went down but my right shin bears the loose-board battle scar, about five inches long. And as I was crouched there in an Olympic sprinter's position, Silas called out a word of warning that no doubt he's repeated many times to un-suspecting, and uninvited, visitors: "Watch oiut for that first step! It ain't nailed down!"

I swallowed the reply that immediately came to mind, got up, and busied myself rubbing my right shin as I balanced on my left leg.

"Been meanin' to fix that step," he said. "The thing's been loose for nigh on to three years now, but ever'time I get set to fix it the fish seem to be bitin' or somethin' else comes up."

"More lak five or six," Nellie countered without looking up, still rocking.

"Well, it *is* a little dan-gerous," I said. "Somebody could get hurt bad."

"Yep, I reckon so," Silas agreed. "Don't never step on it, m'sef. Course, me an' Nellie both know 'bout it an'

we don't have much comp'ny. But I'm gonna' fix it one o' these days."

"Yeah? When?" asked Nellie, still rocking, but at a noticeably slower tempo.

"Oh, one o' these days. I'll git 'round to it," Silas promised, but didn't sign nothing binding.

"Yeah, I bet ya' will," said Nellie, who had stopped rocking.

I got my directions and left, figuring the loose-step argument fuse had been lit, and it was probably a short one.

As I drove home I pondered Silas's statement, "I'm gonna' fix it one o' these days," and the old quotation, "The road to hell is paved with good intentions." I rubbed my sore shin and almost became angry with Silas. But by the time I arrived at my house some six hours later, I had changed my mind about him and his loose board. Here's why.

We are so quick to criticize the inaction of others while things that need attention around our own houses go wanting. Take my house for instance:

• I've lived in it for almost seven years, and out back

there is a piece of pipe sticking up out of the ground about four inches. It represents the remains of a clothesline erected by the previous owner who took the clothesline with him but left the pipe behind. I can't recall ever going in my backyard that I didn't stumble over that piece of pipe, and every time I do it I blame the previous owner, direct a few choice words his way, and vow to "fix it one of these days."

• I have a navy blue blazer with the top front button missing. The button is in the left pocket and has been resting in there since 1982. Every time I wear it I gaze down repeatedly and tell myself, "I'm gonna' get that button sewed on one o' these days."

• My kitchen stove hasn't worked since 1983. Something about a fuse or a relay, or somethin'. I only think about it when I get ready to boil some corn on the cob or have a cravin' f'r grits. But "I'm gonna' get it fixed one o' these days."

• I have a window fan in my bedroom. The breeze feels so good when it blows across my bed late at night and early in the morning.

Something happened to it in the summer of '84, so I've been sleepin' on the sofa in the lobby at the radio station across the street since then. It really don't sleep bad, but "I'm gonna' get that darn fan fixed one o' these days."

• The margins on my typewriter don't work—haven't for years. Can't set 'em, and the result is that I get carried away sometimes and type a line all the way into my carport. But you can bet your correction tape that "I'm gonna' get the thing fixed one o' these days."

• I also have a favorite pair of gray slacks that I like to wear with my one-button navy blue blazer. It seems that I only reach for them when I have but a few minutes to get dressed, get to a speech commitment, a funeral, or to my Sunday school when it's fourth Sunday and my turn to teach.

The problem is that for the past couple of years the zipper has been stuck—down! I'll tell you, it's downright uncomfortable to walk around all day in a crouched position like maybe your back's broken or you're looking for the first available keyhole. But one thing for sure, "I'm gonna' get that zipper fixed . . . one o' these days."

Silas, I'll make you a deal. I'll step over your bottom step if you'll overlook that land mine in my backyard, my navy blue blazer, my inoperative kitchen stove, my broken bedroom window fan, the injured margin setter on my typewriter, and the busted zipper on my gray slacks.

Or maybe, just maybe, I could work out a deal with Nellie to fix my zipper in exchange for a repair job on that bottom step.

WE SOUTHERNERS VALUE OUR PRIVACY

One couple who had retired to the South from Cleveland, Ohio, after purchasing a small farm in South Alabama learned quickly the independence, outspokenness, and conservative ways of at least two of their new neighbors shortly after arriving in Alabama. Both concluded that it would be a good idea to get out on a Sunday afternoon and visit some of their neighbors, exchange greetings, and generally get to know them.

This they did, and they made their first stop at a modest farm home featuring a porch. It was mid-afternoon on a hot Alabama July day, and the man and wife of the house were both sitting in high-back rocking chairs, the only chairs on the porch. The old man was chewing tobacco while his wife was dipping snuff. Both held and waved funeral home hand-held fans, primarily to ward off the pesty gnats common to South Alabama.

The newly settled-in couple just-arrived-from-Cleveland got out of their automobile and approached the house, stepping around one hound dog and over two others. They stopped at the bottom of the front porch steps, and the Cleveland man opened what would be a short conversation with, "Hello there! My wife and I just moved in about two miles down the road a few days ago. We moved down from Cleveland and drove down this afternoon to speak with you, visit and become acquainted."

"Howdy," replied the old man in the rocking chair as he drenched a dead petunia with tobacco juice just to the

left of a broken syrup bottle in the yard.

The old lady never looked up, continuing to rock and sew on what appeared to be a napkin. Like her husband, she took a snuff juice shot at a geranium just off the end of the porch near a lazy cat. She missed the geranium but scored a bull's-eye on the cat's back.

The visitor, still standing with his wife, made another attempt at familiarity with, "Sure is warm this after-noon, isn't it?"

The old man saturated a fern this time before answer-ing with, "Yep, always is this time o' year."

Becoming increasingly im-patient, and a little bit perturbed at the reception he and his wife were receiving, the visitor remarked, "Seems to me like you don't have enough chairs."

"Got plenty o' chairs," the old man said, "just got too much dadblamed comp'ny."

WISDOM IN THE COUNTRY STORE

I guess every small town in America has its own philosophers, and the South has more than its share, I reckon.
Year after year, generation after generation, they spin their
yarns and advance their ideas in the little stores and shops
where people gather. I remember some of them as a boy
growing up in South Georgia.

In Alma there was Lee's Drug Store, on the corner, naturally. The philosopher in residence was one "Shack" Roberts.
I never knew his first name.

In Oglethorpe there was Dan Kleckley's Grocery, next to the
courthouse. The resident philosopher there was Col. J. J. Bull,
a lawyer, whose office was across the street next to Taylor's
Drug Store.

In Lumpkin the philosophers gathered in front of the
Singer Company to eat peanuts, drink Cokes, and discuss
world affairs. My daddy was a regular there, along with Jeff
and Sam Singer.

In Metter the gathering spot was Franklin Chevrolet, with
George Franklin and "Red" Henderson leading the discus-
sions.

In Reynolds it was Goddard's General Store, with Ed Goddard chairing the morning sessions.

I could go on and on about such places and the gems of
wisdom I picked up at them. Gems like these:

"Never trust a man who don't stand up when 'Dixie' is
being played."

"Never trust a man who don't eat grits."

"Never trust a man who repeatedly claims he's overworked
and underpaid."

Never is the key word, and here are a few more gems of wisdom that come to mind. These are definitely taboo:

- Never shake hands with a policeman while wearing brass knuckles.
- Never let yourself be caught within ten blocks of any high school when it lets out.
- Never order a "Little Mac" at McDonald's.
- Never wear a coonskin cap to a Moose Club.
- Never buy a frozen food franchise in Alaska.
- Never dance while wearing golf shoes.
- Never buy instant coffee on the lay-away plan.
- Never buy anything that has to be assembled.
- Never buy anything that contains a sheet of paper that says, "Just Follow These Simple Instructions."
- Never order chitlins at Nikolai's Roof or quiche at Buster's Barbeque.
- Never wear flip-flops to a wedding.
- Never pick up a porcupine with your bare hands.
- Never ask the boss if you can have a coffee break if you're employed at Lipton Tea Co.
- Never make an ugly face at a Doberman.
- Never play the trumpet while chewing gum.

- Never eat Georgia grits with Chinese chopsticks.
- Never drink hot tea or iced coffee. The Lord never intended it that way.
- Never eat in any cafe that serves foreign food.
- Never order barbeque in any establishment that serves anything else.
- Never let nobody from nowhere make fun of the way you talk.
- Never loan your knife, shotgun, or pickup to nobody.
- Never turn your back on any man wearing an earring.
- Never run when you can walk.
- Never walk when you can ride.
- Never stand up when you can sit down.
- Never sit down when you can lie down.
- Never wear anything chartreuse or lavender.
- Never forget your wife's birthday.
- Never eat no meat that ain't fried.
- Never pass up an opportunity to praise the South.
- Never wear lace-up boots when you have athlete's foot.
- Never love a stranger. Be sure and get the name first.
- Never stick chewing gum behind your ear.
- Never wear knickers in public.
- Never criticize the farmer while your mouth's full of food.
- Never strike a match to check the contents of your gas tank.
- Never play poker with a man wearing long sleeves.
- Never try to throw a boomerang away.
- Never take a mother's love for granted.

AN UPDATE ON OLE ROBBIE NAIL BAIL

It's amazing how we run into people at the darnedest places. Like last week when I stopped at the Yo-Ho Inn Beer Joint and Transmission Repair on U.S. 1 between Lyons and Baxley to make a telephone call. The last person in the world I expected to run into there was Robbie Nell Bell, from Alma ("Robbie Nail Bail, fum Almer"), my old redneck friend.

I recognized Robbie Nail as soon as I entered the Yo-Ho Inn. She was shooting eight-ball with Boozer, and munching on a beef jerky. I was careful not to speak to her until the game was over. Robbie Nail "don't lack to be messed with" when she's shootin' pool.

She banked the eight ball in the side pocket, hung up her cue stick, and picked up a wrinkled dollar that Boozer had dropped on the table.

"Thanks, Turkey," she said to Boozer.

"Hey, Goat! Gimme a longneck Bud an' be dang sure it's cold," she said, dropping Boozer's buck on the bar.

"Y' ain't paid f'r that jerky yet," Goat said.

"Ain't goin' to, neither. Not as much money as I put in that jukebox an' cigarette machine. An' 'nother thang—if'n you don't lack it just say so an I'll start goin' to th' Yeller Liver Bar on th' river," she threatened.

"Aw, Robbie Nail. I's jus' teasin', you know that," Goat said, almost apologetically.

"Ya' dang well better be. Hell, I've passed up better places 'n this lookin' f'r a ladies' room," she grumbled, moving toward the front door. "An' take that quarter change an' play Q-2, Goat."

I called to her just as she reached the door. "Hey! Robbie Nail!"

She turned, spotted me

standing by the telephone, and tossed her empty long-neck Bud bottle in the general direction of a trash can.

"Hey, newspaper man! Whut th' heck're ya' doin' daoun heah in God's country?" she asked.

"Oh, just passing through on my way back to Dublin," I told her. "What're you doing here? Last time I saw you, you were working at Mel's down near Broxton."

"Still do. I'm jus' up here f'r th' pageant Sat'day night in Lyons," she said.

"Pageant? What kind of pageant?"

"Miss Georgia Redneck. Havin' th' state finals at th' Red Barn Sat'day night," she said.

"Are you in it?"

"Dang right, good buddy. I'm representin' Region Four as Miss South Georgia Redneck," she boasted.

"Well! Congratulations, Robbie Nail! That's great and . . ."

"Shhhh! Don't call me that," she cautioned in a whisper.

"Why not? That's your name, right?"

"Yeah, right. But las' year's winner, Johnnie Faye Ramsey, said I'd be better off

to use jus' one name. She won with 'Faye' so I'm jus' usin' plain 'Nail,' O.K.?"

"Sure, fine. Nail it is," I promised.

"I 'prechate it. Now then . . . Hey, Goat! What happened to my dadgummed song? I tol' ya' to play Q-2 an' you played J-2. Wha's goin' on?" Robbie Nail demanded.

"I jus' made a mistake."

"Yeah? Well, you're gonna' make another'n if'n ya' don' put in 'nother quarter 'n play Q-2. Ya' heah that?" she warned.

In a matter of seconds the jukebox was blaring out with "Now I Lay Me Down to Cheat," by David Allen Coe.

"Jus' plain don' lack J-2," she mumbled.

"What is J-2?" I asked.

"'Your Bedroom Eyes' by Vern Gosdin. Too sad. Makes me cry."

(I didn't pursue the point but couldn't help but muse on what she'd said. I'd give my twelve-string guitar, two Webb Pierce albums, and a Merle Haggard tape to see Robbie Nail Bail cry.)

I inquired further into the Region Four Miss Redneck Pageant.

"Where was the pageant held, Robbie Nail?"

"In Raymond Braswell's cow barn 'bout three miles out fum Broxton."

"Was it a beauty contest, or what?" I asked.

"Partly, but the mos' important thang was the talent. Least tha's what th' judges said."

"Who won the talent competition?"

"I did. Tha's th' main reason I'm here," she bragged.

"What'd you do, sing?"

"Sang? Hell, I can't sang. I changed all four tires on Junior Blakely's stock car and filled 'er up with gas in twenty-three seconds flat. New record," she said.

"Well, didn't Mildred Walters win last year?"

"Yeah . . . but she got disqualified during the questioning this year."

"Disqualified? Why?

"Oh, one o' them smart aleck judges ast her right in front of ever'body how often she procrastinated, an' that done it, friend," Robbie Nail explained.

"What do you mean? What did Mildred do?"

"Do? She flattened that sucker with a right and then stomped on his face till th' sheriff stopped her. An' I tell you, I don't blame her a dadgummed bit. We didn' none of us get in th' pageant to be insulted."

NEVER TRUST A MAN WHO RUNS WHEN HE DON'T HAVE TO

On my way to visit my publisher recently, I stopped briefly at a country store on the outskirts of Tullahoma, Tennessee. I had a craving for a Coca-Cola and found one there in a six-ounce bottle. Delicious! I burped all the way to Manchester, thirty-five miles to the north.

While the Coca-Cola was refreshing, the conversation I overheard between two Tennesseans in the store was even more so. I guess it was because I heard the owner of the store use a word that I can't recall hearing since my grandfather, Wes Whaley, died in 1944. He also owned a country store, in Powelton, the entire contents of which would easily have fit in a supermarket shopping cart.

The word? *Leery.* The Tennessee store owner used the word *leery* as he explained why he had refused to cash a check for a stranger who had just left.

"Can't quite put my finger on it, George, but I was just a li'l bit leery of him," he said.

Well, as I burped and motored on toward Nashville I pondered the word. I guess we're all a little bit leery of certain individuals at times. I know I am. And like the store owner in Tullahoma, I can't quite put my finger on the reason why.

For instance, I know I'm leery of:

• Any man who wears sunglasses inside during the daytime.

• Any man who can strike a kitchen match with his thumbnail or on the seat of his pants.

• Any man who wears an earring.

• Any man who wears his wristwatch with the face of the watch on the inside of his wrist.

• Any man who wears a

118

pinkie ring.

- Any man who wears his belt with the buckle pointed toward first or third base.
- Any man who wears sideburns down to his jawbone.
- Any man who keeps his wallet in his front pants pocket.
- Any man who wears toe-grip sandals in public.
- Any man who reads his horoscope before turning to the sports page.
- Any man who drinks hot tea or iced coffee.
- Any man who makes change from the collection plate.
- Any man who peeks during the Sunday morning prayer.
- Any man who watches "The Donahue Show."
- Any man who doesn't remove his hat when dining with a lady.
- Any man who strikes a match utilizing a stroke *away* from his body.
- Any man who spits on the sidewalk.
- Any man who refuses to pay his child support.
- Any man who doesn't eat grits.
- Any man who can negotiate I–285 on the first try.
- Any man who keeps his cigarettes rolled up in the sleeve of his T-shirt.
- Any man who wears his cap backwards.
- Any man who takes two parking spaces.
- Any man who breaks in line.
- Any man who understands the metric system, or celsius.
- Any man who smacks when he eats or grits his teeth when he sleeps.
- Any man (or woman) who pops chewing gum.
- Any man whose favorite colors are chartreuse and lavender.
- Any man who reads a newspaper while playing poker.
- Any man who sleeps in church.
- Any man who runs when he doesn't have to.
- Any man who repeatedly states how religious, patriotic, or wealthy he is.
- Any man who doesn't know all the words to "Dixie" and doesn't stand up when he hears it played.
- Any man who wears his sunglasses on top of his head.
- Any man who constantly jingles the change in his pocket.
- Any man who can re-

fold a road map to its original state.

• Any man who works in a flower bed when he could be playing golf.

• Any man who can assemble a swing set on the first try.

• Any man from north of Nashville.

• Any man who speaks more than one language.

• Any man who "dogears" book pages.

• Any man who works crossword puzzles with a ballpoint pen.

• Any man who says to me, "Boy! Have I got a deal for you."

Nope, while I can't put my finger on it—I'm just leery of 'em.

THE LAND OF BUMPER STICKERS

The Southland is the home of bumper stickers. The more I ride the highways and byways the more of them I see. Wouldn't you think the bumper sticker authors would run dry after a while? Not so. There are some catchy ones gracing rear bumpers all over America and here are some that made it to the rear bumpers down here:

- "If you get any closer—introduce yourself."
- "If you can read this—thank a teacher."
- "My wife is driving my Rolls Royce."
- "U toucha my car—İ breaka you face!" (New York license plate).
- "Please tailgate—I need the money."
- "Feeling sick? See your lawyer."
- "Boycott farmers—don't eat!"
- "Prune juice makes the going good!!!"
- "I found it!"
- "I lost it!"
- "I bought it!"
- "I sold it!"
- "I stole it!"
- "I STEPPED IN IT!"
- "CAUTION: Leg check 50 yards ahead!"
- "Women belong in the House—and in the Senate!"
- "Joan of Arc is alive and medium-well!"
- "Just because I'm paranoid, doesn't mean they're not after me."
- "I'm a virgin." (This is a very old bumper sticker.)
- "WARNING: Trespassers will be violated."
- "Support mental health or I'll kill you!"
- "ATTENTION DOCTORS: Firemen make housecalls."
- "Save energy—sleep closer."
- "Remember the Alimony."
- "Bring back the 60s."

121

- "I is a journalist."
- "Individualists of the world—Unite!"
- "CAUTION: Adults playing."
- "Kissing a smoker is like licking an ashtray!"
- "55 MPH is creepy."
- "Go ahead and hit me—my brother's an attorney."
- "Chicken Little was right!"
- "Vote 'YES' on Preparation H!"
- "The Ayatollah is an old meanie!"
- "Pray for me—I drive the freeway daily."
- "The person who has everything should be quarantined!"
- "A bigamist is one who keeps two himself!"
- "How many leaves did Eve try on before she said, 'I'll take this one.'"
- "My husband is a great lover—and if I ever catch him at it I'll kill him!"
- "Lower the age of puberty!"
- "Where there's a pill there's a way!"
- "Two can live as cheaply as one what?"
- "Elevator operators never get to hear the end of the story."
- "Join the Marines—intervene in the country of your choice!"
- "Want a youthful figure? Ask a woman her age."
- "It still takes two to make a marriage—a girl and her mother!"
- "You're never too old to yearn."
- "Remember, some stretch pants have no choice."
- "A bird in the hand can be an awful mess!"
- "If at first you don't succeed—so much for sky diving."
- "Our generation was brought up on the wrong side of the tax."
- "Ban bumper stickers!"

NO SPEAKA DA ENGLISH SOUTH OF FORT PIERCE

I just took the bull by the horns a few months back and decided to tour Florida. After all, having been its neighbor for 45 of my 60 years, I thought it would be a good idea. What the heck, don't people from New Jersey visit New York; and don't Californians visit Nevada with regularity? What about folks in Minneapolis and St. Paul? I'll bet they visit. So why shouldn't a Georgia boy pay a visit to Florida? I took two weeks off and did just that.

My tour took me to Jacksonville, St. Augustine, Daytona Beach, Orlando (Epcot and Disneyworld), Cape Canaveral (Kennedy Space Center), Fort Pierce, West Palm Beach, Fort Lauderdale, and Miami.

My ten-day vacation in Florida proved to be quite a learning experience and I'm sharing my experiences here with the realization that many of you who read this book will sooner or later tour the Sunshine State and spend some time in the cities I visited.

Here are some of the things I learned:

- It is absolutely against the law for anyone who speaks English to work as a motel desk clerk in Florida.

- There are exactly 1,047,313 fast food restaurants between Brunswick, Georgia, and Miami, Florida.

- For every fast food restaurant there are at least two condominium complexes, each laying claim to being the best deal in Florida.

- Everything in Florida from Cokes to condos is 50 percent overpriced.

- There is a continuing contest in Florida among women of all ages to see how little clothing they can wear without being arrested. And the men buy Murine by

the gallon.

• There are more T-shirts in Florida than in Taiwan and Korea combined.

• Every motel is after the senior citizen dollar, all having senior citizens clubs with different names.

• St. Augustine really *is* an old city. Everything in it is old. Heck, radio stations there don't even begin announcing birthdays until the celebrant reaches 80—and then the song they play most is Nat King Cole's "Too Young."

• Interstate-9 is a boring ride. All there is to do is listen to the radio and read. I read "The Rise and Fall of the Third Reich" and "War and Peace" between Daytona Beach and Fort Lauderdale.

• Nobody speaks English south of Fort Pierce.

LOVE IT HERE BY TURKEY CREEK

Real, bonafide and planned vacations have never played a very big part in my life. But I did take one once, for two whole weeks in 1962. That wound me up. The best part of the whole thing was the three days I had when I got back home in New Jersey before going back to work in New York. I decided that summer that I would conform and do like some eleven million other people in New York and New Jersey do—pack up and head for Florida. I did, and that was the last vacation I took. Here's why:

I left New Jersey in a non-air-conditioned 1960 Chevrolet, packed to the headliner with luggage, snacks, soft drinks, a wife, a ten-year-old son, a four-year-old daughter, a year-old puppy of questionable ancestry and enough games and toys to open my own toy store. And, there were no interstate highways. I fought cars of various descriptions on roads and highways that would be condemned by today's standards.

To the best of my recollection, I didn't pass up a "baffroom" between Roselle Park, New Jersey, and Fernandina Beach, Florida; and once we arrived I spent ten days with sand in my undershorts, as well as shaving with, bathing in, and drinking water that smelled like a cross between rotten eggs and sulphur. I financed the purchase of enough boardwalk junk to fill a cotton warehouse and cut bubble gum from my daughter's hair twice before she ever got into the ocean.

On the return trip we renewed acquaintances with all the owners of public "baffrooms" we'd met ten days earlier, boosted bubble gum stock to the point of splitting and declaring twin dividends. I had neglected to purchase the two visible symbols so closely associated with automobiles bearing New Jersey license plates that satisfies all the neighbors when you return home that you have indeed been to Florida on vacation: one bag each of Indian River oranges and grapefruit. But I got lucky and found a bag of each at a fruit stand on the outskirts of Dover, Delaware, bought them at armed robbery prices, and placed them strategically in the rear window for full viewing when I pulled into my driveway. (Both children had been bribed with my last remaining two one-dollar bills in exchange for a promise of secrecy regarding the origin of the oranges and grapefruit.)

I thought about that 1962 vacation(?) at length recently when I read a newspaper story saying that most of my fellow Georgians would prefer to leave Middle Georgia for vacations. I just can't agree. I would be hard put to pick up and leave Middle Georgia to go on vacation anywhere. Here's why:

I am writing this while sitting on the bank of Turkey Creek, as close to nature as I can get. Even as I type I can hear the sound water makes as it rolls over a bed of maybe 500 huge rocks below me in Turkey Creek. I see busy squirrels and romping rabbits scampering around. I see nervous birds moving from tree to tree. I hear the constant and never-ending sound of crystal-clear water from an artesian well not five feet away splashing on more rocks in Turkey Creek. Add to this a brisk breeze that caresses my face and blows my papers, bright sunshine that reflects off the water below and a caring God that watches over all this. And there are three excellent golf courses within ten minutes.

Thanks to a very good friend, I enjoy the good life on the banks of Turkey Creek several days a week when I come here to write. He said the magic words when he told me this about his recently constructed "cabin" in the woods. "You are welcome to come here as often as you like, spend the night if you care to, just enjoy it."

It scares me at times when I pause to consider the good life I enjoy in Middle Georgia because I'm not sure I deserve it. But I love it and enjoy it.

Leave Middle Georgia? No, thanks. I've got it made here, and I know it. In winter I'll just move my computer inside, put on a pot of coffee, and hope it rains.

GEORGIA VACATIONS ARE GREAT

I'll never understand why so many people are hell-bent to leave Georgia to vacation in such places as England, France, Germany, Italy, Holland, Sweden, and Denmark. Or to China, Israel, Japan, Canada, Mexico or some other foreign country like New York, New Jersey, or Miami.

I sat in the Atlanta airport recently waiting for a passenger to arrive from Nashville. While waiting I watched passengers debark from a Miami to Atlanta flight, and loved the sticker on one passenger's shoulder bag: "Will The Last American To Leave Miami Please Bring The Flag."

Of the foreign countries listed above, I've only traveled to four of them—Mexico, New York, New Jersey, and Miami. And I ain't got no immediate plans to go back no time soon. I can get all the vacationing I want right here in Georgia where English is spoken and grits are served. And don't try to tell me about them sissy grits—cream of wheat. I figure that anybody who will eat cream of wheat will use a cigarette holder, drink hot tea and iced coffee, and eat pumpernickel bread on purpose. Trust me, friend, I'm convinced the Good Lord never intended for us to do things like that.

A favorite Georgia vacation spot of mine is St. Simons, the playground of the rich. Most are from up North and bed down at The Cloister Hotel where wake-up calls don't even start until 11 A.M. I did stay at The Cloister once—for three days—and filed for Chapter 11 as soon as I returned home. Only rich Yankees, and maybe a few rich widows, can afford The Cloister. The bootleggers and doctors not being sued for malpractice stay at the minor league hotel, the King and Prince. I grant you it's in the high minor leagues, but compared to The Cloister it's still not in the majors.

I usually stay at the Queen's Court, semi-pro, but eat breakfast at the King and Prince. Breakfast is my main meal, and the Good Lord intended when he put us here that everybody eat a good breakfast. My grandmother said so, and breakfast at the King and Prince is great.

The last time I had breakfast there I had a window table overlooking the ocean. At 7:30 A.M., a bunch of Yankees were walking on the beach, not because they were enjoying it but because other Yankees who came before 'em said you were supposed to.

Now then, eating breakfast at the King and Prince ain't just eating breakfast—it's a happening. I helped myself to the buffet and returned to my window table loaded down with fresh cantaloupe, strawberries, corn flakes, eggs fried medium like the Good Lord intended for eggs to be fried, grits, bacon and homemade biscuits. And the waitress had re-filled my coffee cup, bless her heart. Ummmmm . . . the eggs were so fresh that I could have sworn I saw the hen that laid them tip-toe from the kitchen and exit through a

side door, her day's work done. The biscuits? I bit into one and tuned my ear to the kitchen in the event my grandmother, a world champion biscuit maker, might be in there kneading dough and singing "Amazing Grace."

For more than an hour I enjoyed a delicious breakfast. All finished, I desperately wanted to burp in a vocal gesture of satisfaction to one and all. I refrained. Heck, a fella' don't even dare sneeze at the King and Prince or The Cloister, let alone burp. I waited until I was out on the beach.

I did go for a walk on the beach after breakfast. I figured I was supposed to. The Yankees had disappeared by the time I got there, no doubt into the King and Prince to read the *New York Times*. (St. Simons and Sea Island may well be the only places in Georgia where the *New York Times* is the dominant newspaper.) Mentioning St. Simons and Sea Island in the same breath is like comparing flat sardines to caviar, or Flatbush Avenue to Park Avenue.

I walked for a little while and then sat on the beach, and while sitting there Libya and Khadafy seemed so remote, having been temporarily replaced by the peace and tranquility that prevail in St. Simons. And everybody's equal there—the New Jersey real estate magnate, the New York stockbroker, the rich man's son from Boston, the rich widow from Delaware, the Minnesota doctor, the South Georgia bootlegger, and a small-town newspaper columnist from Dublin, Georgia.

I sat there with sand between my toes, the wind in my hair, the sun in my face, and surrounded by Yankees. I realized that, for the moment at least, we all shared a common address—"The King and Prince Hotel, St. Simons Island, Georgia 31522."

And I learned something, too. Yankees ain't all that bad, and you can love 'em if you just get to know 'em.

THE ROAD TO AFFLUENCE AIN'T EASY

It matters not where your roots are, there's not a man alive who doesn't dream of one day reaping the fruits of his labor and make for himself and his family a better life. To be able to afford a better car, send his children to better schools, and own a house in a better neighborhood—that's what dreams are made of.

Two prime examples of this immediately come to mind, one concerning a man of the soil from the deep South and another concerning a hard working factory man from the metropolitan and heavily industrialized Detroit area.

First, the farmer from Central Alabama. . . .

The man was no stranger to hard work. He had been on a handshaking basis with it all his life, having been born the son of a sharecropper. He knew about life as a poor boy on an Alabama farm: rising early, before daylight, to help his Daddy with the daily chores that go along with farm life, milking the cows, slopping the hogs, feeding the mules, and cutting stovewood. All this before walking to a one-room schoolhouse and walking back in the afternoon to take up where he'd left off that morning. He did manage to complete the third grade.

After working hard for many years as a sharecropper, he managed to buy a small farm of his own. He was a good farmer, worked long hours and saw his acreage increase over the years from 60 to 80, then to 115 and on to 425. As his acreage increased so did his cows and hogs, and his two mules gave way to big, modernized tractors and combines. He would be characterized as a hard-working, successful farmer.

One day, the day his youngest son graduated from high school, he thought long and hard about his farm and how proud he was of what he had accomplished. On the other hand, he was concerned about its future. His two older sons had expressed no interest in farming. One had gone on to become a successful insurance salesman, and the other had chosen to be a career Army man. But his youngest had displayed a knack for farming, was active in the Future Farmers of America in high school, and had never mentioned pursuing any other career.

After graduation, the farmer sat his son down and explained to him that the farm would one day be his and he would like the boy to go to college, major in agriculture, and come back and help him run the farm. The boy agreed and enrolled in the University of Alabama to study agriculture.

One day, after having completed his second year at the university, the boy approached his father in the vicinity of the hogpen and told him he'd like to talk with him about his education and his future. Both sat on a rail fence as they talked. The boy spoke first.

"Daddy, I've been in college for two years now and I've decided I don't want to study agriculture no more."

"Whadda' you mean, boy? You done half way through already an' now you say you wanna' quit," the father said.

"No sir, I don't wanna' quit college. I jus' don't wanna' study agriculture," the boy explained. "I wanna' study medicine an' be a doctor and. . . ."

"Study medicine an' be a doctor? Boy, we ain't runnin' no doctor place heah. We runnin' a farm an' I need you to learn how to raise corn and soybeans, raise cows an' hogs an' come back heah an' hep me run this heah farm," the father said.

"But Daddy, I wanna' study medicine, an' be a doctor," the boy persisted. "An' I wanna' specialize."

"Specialize? What're you talkin' 'bout now?"

"Yes, sir, I wanna' be a doctor an' specialize in ostastesticks."

"Ostastesticks? Naw, you ain't gonna' waste yo' time an' my money studyin' no ostastesticks."

"But why not? Ostastesticks is a good field and. . . ."

"Now you listen to me,

boy. Jus' as sho' as you spend all that time an' money learnin' 'bout that ostastesticks some smart aleck will come along and find a cure fo' it an' then you'll be out of a job!"

Then, there was the fellow from Michigan who retired after putting in 27 long and hard years in a Detroit factory. He took his life's savings, moved to Florida, and bought a house with a swimming pool, in a very affluent neighborhood. All his working years he had dreamed of having a house with a swimming pool.

The neighborhood in which he bought his house was infested with doctors. In fact, 90 percent of those living in the subdivision were doctors, all with houses sporting swimming pools, and he learned quickly that a nightly ritual was midnight skinny-dipping. He watched and listened nightly from his patio, and shortly before midnight every night he could see naked bodies sailing off rooftops and hear the resounding "splashes" that followed.

One hot July night as he sat and listened, he decided to join in the fun. You know, become one of the gang inasmuch as he and his wife had not, up to that time, received the warmest of receptions from his new neighbors. So he peeled off his T-shirt and shorts and struggled to his roof. Weighing in at just over 300 pounds, it was no easy task. But he finally made it, and there he stood on his roof above his pool as naked as the day he clocked into this world up in Michigan.

He was so excited about what he was preparing to do that it never crossed his mind that he had never bothered to learn how to swim. Sure enough, he sailed off his roof and performed a perfect belly-buster into his pool. Water splashed rooftop high, causing his next door neighbor, an inhalation and respiratory specialist who weighed in at 127 pounds, great alarm. He peered through his redwood fence and realized immediately that his neighbor was in trouble, waving his arms frantically and shouting, "Help! I can't swim!"

By the time the specialist arrived, his neighbor had gone under twice and was strangling and choking. He jumped into the pool and by

some miracle succeeded in getting the heavyweight to the edge of the pool, but he was unable to lift him out. Only his head and arms were resting on the edge of the pool. The remainder of his body was still underwater, and he continued to cough and sputter as the specialist began to administer artificial respiration.

The specialist was working frantically, and each time he pressed down on his neighbor's upper back a stream of water spurted from his mouth. Nevertheless, the determined specialist

continued, unaware that he was being observed by a man, dressed in coveralls, leaning against the corner of the house and eating an apple—until he spoke:

"You're doing that all wrong, you know," the observer remarked between bites on his apple.

"What? All wrong?" said the specialist as he continued to press down on his neighbor's back and release, with the stream of water spurting from his mouth with each depression.

"Right, all wrong."

"I'll have you know that I

specialized in inhalation and respiratory medicine in medical school, and have been in practice here for 18 years now," the specialist explained between pushes.

"Don't make no difference. You're still doin' it all wrong," said the apple eater.

"Oh yeah? Well, who are you? Are you a doctor?"

"Nope, I'm a plumber, and I can tell you one thing for sure. If you don't get that guy's tail out of the water, you're gonna' pump the pool dry!"

SECTION SEVEN

SOUTHERN VIEWPOINTS

A WORD OF EXPLANATION

No doubt you will notice that this section is a little different than the rest of the book. Up to now everything I've written has been to help the sons and daughters of the South understand Northerners—and to help Yankees understand us Southerners. Some of it may even help us understand ourselves a bit more.

I'm widening my horizons a little in this section, however, to include some observations on life in general. Life these days is moving faster than a coon dog on fresh tracks, and if we can just set back a little and think about what's happening it will provide us with many ironic, pleasant moments.

That's what I've tried to do in this section. I've had some fun at the expense of the world around me, and I've concluded that whether our world is good or bad depends on how we let it affect us. Let's face it. An awful lot of what's going on today is extremely funny if we will just make the effort to think about it.

Someone once said that the more things change, the more they stay the same. That's true. But it's also true that the more things change, the more they change!

So that's what this section is all about. Things that change and things that stay the same. And while I haven't consciously tried to say, "This is how a Southerner thinks," I certainly have thought as one as I have written.

QUESTIONS I'D LIKE SOMEONE TO ANSWER

After reading Lewis Grizzard's *If Love Were Oil, I'd Be About A Quart Low*, I'm seriously considering writing a sequel, *If Love Were Oil, It Wouldn't Make A Mark On My Dipstick*.

I don't normally waste my valuable time poring over such trivial scribblings, but I like Grizzard and did enjoy his book and bought a few for Christmas presents.

I usually dwell on such delicate and vital matters as "Who really killed Cock Robin?" or "What is Rudolph's last name?" And I'm still trying to figure out "Where the yellow went."

No, my time is too valuable to squander it on inconsequential matters regarding Grizzard's oil level. There are many, many questions of world significance yet to be answered, and I dwell on them constantly.

Like these that I'd greatly appreciate your help with. The world is waiting for an answer from intellectuals like you and me.

- Who winds the watch used on CBS's "60 Minutes"?
- Where does Webster look when *he* needs a definition?
- What holds up a strapless gown?
- Whatever happened to the nine-digit ZIP code?
- Did Robin Hood and Jesse James have bank accounts?
- Who hears the Pope's confession?
- In a two-child family, one boy and one girl, which is the opposite sex?
- Who edits what the editor writes?
- Whatever happened to Alice Lon?
- What was Daisy Mae's maiden name?
- Who killed John Wilkes

Booth?

• Does Perry Como take Nytol?

• What kind of pipe tobacco did Bing Crosby smoke? And did he sing in the shower?

• What does a giraffe take for a sore throat?

• How long was the Camptown Racetrack?

• How many miles per gallon does Richard Petty get?

• What was the name of "The Boston Strangler"?

• What was the name of Tim McCoy's horse?

• What size shoe does Tiny Tim wear?

• When Dolly Parton has a chest cold, does she hurt more than other women?

• Who was Arthur Godfrey's announcer?

• Who assassinated James A. Garfield? William McKinley?

• What was Louis "Satchmo" Armstrong's theme song?

• Does Christine Jorgensen go to the men's or ladies' rest room?

• How deep is the Black Hole of Calcutta?

• What is the name of the bull in the Schlitz Malt Liquor commercials?

• What is the capital of Afghanistan?

• What was the final score of the baseball game in which the Mighty Casey struck out?

• Whatever happened to the 52–20 club?

• What was the name of Dennis the Menace's best friend?

• What was the name of the last song Hank Williams recorded? (Here's the answer, and the only one I'm providing today: "I'll Never Get Out Of This World Alive."

• How many legs does a lobster have?

• What is "Little Richard's" last name?

• What was the name of Eleanor Roosevelt's newspaper column?

• Did Wimpy eat onions on his hamburgers?

• Who was Roy Rogers' first wife?

• What is the color of Ronald McDonald's shoelaces?

• What is the brand name of James Bond's cigarette lighter?

• When is the 1939 World's Fair time capsule scheduled to be opened?

• What was the name of Sad Sack's girlfriend in World War II?

• Who owned the boarding house on "Gunsmoke"?

• What is Aunt Jemima's

real name?

- What was the name of Tom Sawyer's girlfriend? Did Huckleberry Finn have one?

- Whatever happened to Charlie McCarthy, Mortimer Snerd, Effie Clinker and Podine Puffington—Edgar Bergen's dummies?

- How much does a calorie weigh?

These are just a few of the world's questions crying out for an answer. Can you help? Please!

WHATEVER HAPPENED TO THE BURMA—SHAVE SIGNS?

Any time I have the opportunity to relive a boyhood experience I seize upon it. It doesn't take much to ignite my flame of youthful memories.

Like an old piece of weathered and worn board I ran across last year in the woods near McRae, I could barely make out the words printed on it. Many years ago it had been painted red, with white letters in script. I could tell the first two letters were *Bu*. Closer observation determined the second word to be *Shave*. Burma—Shave!

Remember those Burma—Shave signs? I wonder what ever happened to them?

BURMA—SHAVE SIGNS ON THE ROAD TO GRANDMA'S

It was in the thirties, I guess. We'd load up in the old Ford in December to ride from such places as Alma and Oglethorpe to rural Hancock County, near Sparta for a Christmas visit at Grandma's. It was a real experience.

People fly from Atlanta to Los Angeles today in less time than it took us to drive to Grandma's. The only thing they have to look at are clouds. On the ride to Grandma's we had Burma—Shave signs. My Dad has backed up many times because his little boy failed to read the last two signs. My Dad was like that.

Sometimes I think he took the long way just so I could read 'em. And they always seemed to be on a curve, remember?

I just don't know. It seems to me that America lost a little of its make-up with the fading away of Burma—Shave signs. They became extinct at age 38 in 1963. They were born in 1925 on Highway 65 in Minnesota. Only four states never had them: New Mexico, Arizona, Massachussetts, and Nevada. I didn't know that because we didn't travel through those states on the way to Grandma's.

HERE'S A FEW FOR OLD TIMES SAKE

A peach—looks good— with lots of fuzz—but man's no peach—and never was— Burma–Shave.

Don't take the curve—at 60 per—we hate to lose—a customer—Burma–Shave.

Every shaver—now can snore—six more minutes— than before—by using— Burma–Shave.

He played a sax—had no B.O.—but his whiskers scratched—so she let him go—Burma–Shave.

Henry the Eighth—Prince of Friskers—lost five wives—but kept his whiskers—Burma–Shave.

Listen birds—these signs cost money—so roost a while—but don't get

funny—Burma–Shave.

Past schoolhouses—take it slow—let the little—shavers grow—Burma–Shave.

Rip a fender—off your car—send it in—for a half-pound jar—Burma–Shave.

Does your husband—misbehave—grunt and grumble—rant and rave?— shoot the brute—some Burma–Shave.

My man—won't shave— says Hazel Huz—but I should worry—Dora's does— Burma–Shave.

Corny? Maybe. But I can tell you one thing, Whiskers, those little Burma–Shave signs on small boards spaced so they could be read sequentially by motorists passing by sure broke the monotony of the long ride to Grandma's for a little boy anxious to get there. And, they beat the heck out of watching a white line in the center of an expressway.

Thanks Burma–Shave, wherever you are, for entertaining me all the way to Grandma's and back.

LAUNDRYMAT PHILOSOPHERS

The last time I made my regular visit to the laundrymat, as usual I forgot to take anything along to read. Life can be boring just waiting for a coin-hungry machine to grunt and grind its way through the wash, rinse, final rinse, and spin-dry cycles. Then there's the additional ten-minute wait while my pants, shirts, socks, and Fruit-of-the-Looms turn somersaults in hot air.

Near the end of the wash cycle I got up and walked around inside, stopping to stare out a window at nothing in particular, except a few empty cans, food wrappers, a detergent box, and two mismatched socks. But something on the inside caught my eye, the handiwork of wall artists and wall writers, most of which can't be printed here.

I learned, among other things, that Patsy loves Jim, Linda has flipped over Robert, and that Laverne will love Ken until the end of time. And hearts, done in black spray paint and pierced with arrows, were by far the favorites of the artists.

I also learned that Frances from Jacksonville, Joe from Chattanooga, Linda from Detroit, and Natasha from New York have visited Dublin in the past.

I can truthfully say that I have never written anything on a laundrymat or rest room wall, although I'm aware that there are those who feel that's where my stuff belongs. So be it.

It can be frustrating to stand (or sit) and stare at the clever sayings scribbled on a wall and not be able to make a contribution with some one-line epistle. Like, "James Garner really drives a Toyota"; "John Cameron Swayze really wears a Rolex"; "John Madden is really Andy Devine reincarnated"; "Is Lee Iacocca really a chocolate candy bar?" Or maybe a title for Lewis Grizzard's next book, *I Led Three Wives*.

Chances are that some of you have experienced a similar dilemma. Well, fear not. I am going to suggest a few for you that could come in handy. Just clip, save, and stuff them inside your wallet for future reference:

"Where will you spend eternity?"
(Underneath: "The way it looks now, in Algebra 101.")

"Roses are red, violets are blue—always have been, and always will be."

"Tammy loves Henry."
(Underneath: "Great! But the problem is that Henry loves Marie.")

"Go Dawgs!"
(Underneath: "Yeah, go! It don't matter where, just go!")

"Please wash hands before drying."

"Kilroy wouldn't be caught dead in this dump."

"Honolulu is as American as apple poi."

"Mary Poppins has been grounded!"

"Nostalgia ain't what it used to be."

"Bus drivers don't take a back seat to nobody."

"I'd give my right arm to be ambidexterous."

"Albert Einstein was a know-know."

"Help send a girl to Boy's Town."

"A bird in the hand can be real messy."

"Little Bobby Horner sucks his thumb."

"Do not write on walls!"
(Underneath: "What should I do, type?")

"This wall will appear in paperback soon."

"William Tell wore contact lenses."

"The U.N. is alive but dormant."

"W.C. Fields is alive and drunk in Philadelphia."

"Only revolution ends war!"

"Robin Hood was a Ku Klux Klansman."

"How 'bout that Jim Bakker? Can't even spell Baker."

"Nudists wear one-button suits."

"Howard Johnson eats at Kentucky Fried Chicken and licks his fingers!"

"Florence Nightingale was a pan handler."

"Does the Big Top have a Big Bottom?"

"Who pulled the plug?"

"We must silence those who oppose freedom of speech!"

"Repeal the law of gravity."

"John Doe is a nobody."

"You can bet Abraham Lincoln didn't waste HIS time watching television."

"The world is flat."—Class of 1491.

"Lady Godiva wore a fall."

"Mercer coeds are no-shows."

"Wyatt Earp's brother, Virgil, won the showdown at the OK Corral with three kings and a pair of sevens."

"Florists are petal pushers."

"Benjamin Franklin got a charge out of kite flying."

"A beatnick is an exhausted Santa Claus."

"Paul Revere was an alarmist."

"The first book on elephant physiology was written in 1936—this was also the last."

"Evel Knievel is a fall guy."

"The world is coming to an end! Repent! And return those library books."

"I find *Newsweek* easy to digest . . . except for the staples."

"Don't drop out of college!"

(Underneath: "Heavens no! Stay in college and learn to read and riot.")

"God is dead!"—*Time.*

"God is not dead!"—Oral Roberts.

"Who is Oral Roberts?"—God.

WATCH OUT FOR THE OFFICE PARTY

Every year as the office party season runs into high gear, I'm amazed that they go on year after year, with nobody trying to stop them. The annual get-together is the nemesis of the work force that puts the employee in a no-win situation— damned (at home) if he does and damned (at the office) if he doesn't.

Office parties probably break up more marriages, thwart more budding careers, and generally create more trouble than Watergate, Abscam, the Iran–Contra Hearings, the Jim and Jessica $265,000 PTL waltz, an "innocent" cruise to Bimini by an aspiring presidential candidate, stolen quotes by Lyin' Joe Biden, the October Wall Street crash, the Bork and Ginsburg sitcom, and hemorrhoids combined.

So, for those of you forced to attend the monsters, here is a set of ground rules that could save your marriage, your job, and a bondsman's fee:

WHALEY'S OFFICE PARTY RULES

• Abstain from partaking of any liquid in a container bearing the emblem of a Wild Turkey and the number "105," or has an inscription promoting a life of Southern comfort. Both are camouflaged LSD.

• Do not under any circumstances propose marriage within earshot of witnesses.

• Caution: When the keypunch operator with the mole, buck teeth, acne, and Bella Abzug figure begins to resemble Vanna White, excuse yourself, slip into the office infirmary, and lie down for an hour. Apply

145

cold compresses to your forehead.

• Never take a raincoat, umbrella, or a favorite scarf to an office party. Odds are about 15–1 that you'll lose all three.

• Do not "go on to someplace else" when the party finally begins to wind down. Joints with piano bars featuring "Go-Go" girls or "somebody's camphouse" are especially to be avoided.

• Don't tell war stories, especially about your marriage prior to the divorce.

• Never accept a cigarette from anybody in the rest room that has just been rolled by hand, with "tobacco" taken from a little plastic bag that bears a Colombian stamp.

• Should you by chance succeed in luring the office sexpot into a private office, be sure she doesn't activate the "intercom–transmit" button if she's sitting on the desk. And if the red light on the closed circuit TV is "on," by all means move on to another office. "Candid Camera" at office parties can be lethal.

• Never enter any room without knocking first.

• Never, under any circumstances, allow yourself to be photographed with a member of the opposite sex.

• Do not sing. Anyone rejected by the youth choir at age nine rarely develops into a Lee Greenwood or Whitney Houston on a December evening of his or her fortieth year.

• Resist all efforts to be recruited for a spontaneous performance of "A Chorus Line" with trousers rolled up to the knee and arms linked.

• Do not try on a horror mask and blast your noisemaker into the payroll clerk's ear from a distance of nine inches.

• If you are a woman and the guy who works in the mail room who had always reminded you of Buddy Hackett or Don Knotts suddenly takes on the appearance of Robert Redford or Tom Selleck, move briskly and without delay to the break room, apply a cold towel to the back of your neck, and sit down. Drink lots of black coffee if available.

• **Never** take a drunk home from an office party. You do and you can bet your Christmas bonus that his wife will blame you for his condition. And—she'll tell your preacher about it.

• Do not inform the boss's wife that she reminds you of Jessica Hahn or Donna Rice and would make a great *Playboy* centerfold.

• Women should not inquire of male co-workers whether or not they wear Jockey shorts.

• Men should not inquire of female co-workers where they stand on the bra-less issue.

• Do not use ballpoint pens or letter openers for darts to throw at the company founder's portrait in the board room.

• Do not overindulge on the cheese dip or those little sausage balls that simmer in a container with a red hot lid while waiting to be speared with multi-colored toothpicks. As sick as you're going to be the next morning, an empty stomach is infinitely preferable to nausea.

Suggestion: Clip and frame the above. Hang it right between your wedding picture and pictures of the children.

THINGS THAT "TEE ME OFF"

In the past I haven't made New Year's resolutions, but in recent years I've taken a different approach. I'm still not making any, but I do plan to try and be a little more tolerant of those little things in life that "tee me off." You know, pet peeves. We all have them and here are a few of mine that I'm going to try and suppress my complete dislike for, or at least, make an effort to hide my antagonism:

- People who "save seats" at free public events.
- People who break in line.
- Extremely loud car radios or tape players.
- Loud jukeboxes in restaurants.
- Perfectly healthy individuals who park in spaces reserved for the physically handicapped.
- People who get an armload of mail and then sit in their car for an hour in the post office parking lot and open it while cars are backed up to City Hall waiting for a parking place.
- People who repeatedly interrupt.
- People who pop chewing gum in public.
- People who stare . . . and stare . . . and stare.
- Pay toilets. They should all be outlawed.
- People who insist on getting in the supermarket "Six Items or Less" checkout line with enough items to overload a grocery cart.
- Establishments that sell gasoline but provide no rest room facilities for their customers. I avoid them like the plague.
- Cars that sport "On-Board" signs.
- People who take small children into restaurants and then allow them to run wild.

148

● People who sit behind you in the theatre and talk during the entire movie.

● People who block the intersection but won't look at you while doing so.

● People who insist on driving 42 miles per hour and won't budge from the left lane on the expressway.

● People who discard their chewing gum in restaurant ashtrays, underneath theatre seats, and on sidewalks.

● People who straddle the line and take up two parking spaces in crowded parking lots.

● Telephone solicitations of any kind.

● People who appear at my front door on Sunday morning just when I'm shaving and getting ready to go to my church who tell me I'm going straight to hell if I don't believe the way they do.

● People who sit in an adjoining booth and jabber back and forth in a foreign language. (I always get the feeling they're talking about me.)

● Any mail that tells me on the outside of the envelope that I have for sure won a prize, probably worth thousands of dollars.

● Has-been jocks in the broadcast booth who can tell

you exactly why a certain play didn't work—people like John Madden, the Andy Devine clone; Dick Vitale, ESPN's college basketball color man who sports a .50 caliber automatic mouth loaded from a .22 caliber brain; and Beano Cook, whoever the heck he is. And I never thought I would see the day that I'd admit I miss Howard Cossell.

• Women sportscasters who take great pride in their ability to explain a groin injury in minute detail, and the men who do the commercials revealing all the advantages of using a particular feminine hygiene product. You tell me, how do these people know about these things?

• British commentators announcing American golf tournaments.

• Talk show hosts, all of whom believe they're much more important than they really are.

• Dr. Ruth. Take a good look at her and answer me this: How would *she* know about sex?

• John McEnroe. I automatically pull for his opponent, no matter his nationality. McEnroe is a foot-fault in my book.

• Jim and Tammy Faye Bakker. 'Nuff said.

• Bobby Knight, Indiana University basketball embarrassment. I refuse to watch his team play. I'd rather watch Championship Wrestling (and *all* wrestling is Championship Wrestling; the only thing more boring, and predictable, is watching the Braves and the Falcons).

• Joan Rivers. The ol' gal is right where she belongs— going, going, gone!

These are just a few of my pet peeves, and I honestly intend to tolerate or avoid them. I lean toward avoiding them.

SECTION EIGHT

IN CONCLUSION

IF A YANKEE MOVES IN NEXT DOOR

Someone has said, "A man's home is his castle," and this is true. It represents many years of hard work, savings, and labor, and he doesn't want anything or anybody to make waves with it, like maybe routing an interstate highway through the front yard or proposing a hazardous waste dump site in the back one. But what about next door? What if, say, a Yankee moves in next door? What is a man to do?

First, don't panic. Remember that there is a good chance that he didn't move in by choice. Maybe his company transferred him to your town. Maybe he wisely married a Southern girl and is relocating because of that. Southern girls do have a tendency to become homesick at the drop of a boiled peanut, you know.

Here are some suggestions that might help make life easier for everybody concerned if a Yankee moves in next door:

• Don't call the local newspaper and put your house up for sale.

• Don't run to the veterinarian and/or doctor to get inoculated.

• Don't install iron bars over your windows.

• Don't hire a night watchman.

• Don't lock up the dogs and children.

• Don't remove the front porch furniture.

• Don't put in an alarm system or security lights.

• Don't cook chitlins and turn a fan on them in order to blow the stinky smoke in the direction of the new neighbors. (They just might have moved from Secaucus, New Jersey, and odor won't be a problem.)

● Don't "roll" their yard with toilet paper.

● Don't tell the children to "stay away."

These are just a few of the *Don'ts*. Here are a few *Do's* for your consideration:

● Invite them over for a cup of coffee.

● Try and learn as much as possible about them.

● Talk across the backyard fence. Many lasting friendships have begun that way.

● Invite them to attend church with you, or maybe a church supper.

● Take the guy fishing. Whether you catch anything or not is not all that important. I know of no place to get better acquainted than on a river bank or in a bass boat on a lake.

● Invite him to join you after work at the Elk or Moose Lodge for a beer.

● Take him to the morning coffee table. Every town has one and they always welcome new blood.

● Finally, give him the benefit of the doubt. There's a good possibility that he will be an all right guy, and who knows—he might even come to like you.

ROOTS—WILL THE REAL BO WHALEY PLEASE STAND UP?

A few years ago I received a telephone call from the program chairman of a North Carolina civic club to which I had been invited to speak. True to form, he was calling to inquire if I had a resumé and, if so, would I please mail him one as he would be introducing me.

Do I have a resumé? Do insurance agents use rate books? Is New York big? Of course I have a resumé. I wouldn't leave home without it.

After hanging up the telephone, I pulled a copy of my resumé from my file cabinet. I scanned it before mailing it to North Carolina. This is what it looks like and is precisely what the program chairman read when introducing me:

"RESUMÉ OF WALKER W. 'BO' WHALEY"

Born December 11, 1927, Scott, Georgia. Subsequently moved to several South Georgia communities with his parents, his father being a Methodist preacher.

Graduated from Stewart County High School, Lumpkin, Georgia, in May, 1943, and immediately enrolled at Georgia Military College, graduating in December, 1944. Bo was named Most Outstanding Athlete at GMC in both 1943 and 1944.

Inducted into U.S. Army in 1945 and served two years as a combat engineer in the South Pacific before being honorably discharged in November, 1946, and immediately enrolled at Georgia Southern College where he played both varsity baseball

154

and basketball. Graduated in June, 1949, with a BS in History and Physical Education.

Coached baseball and taught history at Georgia Military College from 1949 to 1951. Enrolled in graduate school at George Peabody College, Nashville, Tennessee, receiving the Master of Education degree in 1952.

Coached basketball and baseball and taught history at Dublin, Georgia, High School from 1952 to 1954. Named principal of Wrightsville, Georgia, High School in June, 1954, but prior to the beginning of the school year was appointed a Special Agent of the Federal Bureau of Investigation. He served in this capacity for 21 years in Washington, D.C., Houston, Texas, Detroit, Michigan, Newark, New Jersey, and New York City until his retirement in 1975.

Additionally, from 1949 until 1954, Bo played professional baseball with several minor league teams as a pitcher.

In December, 1977, Bo returned to Dublin, Georgia, to live and began writing a thrice-weekly column for the Dublin *Courier Herald* . . . and still does.

And that, friends and neighbors, is exactly what my resumé says and is what the program chairman read to the North Carolina civic club.

Before driving to North Carolina for my scheduled appearance, I studied my resumé in detail. Remember the television show, "To Tell the Truth?" Well, I thought about it as I read. I concluded that I must do something, so I eased a sheet of paper in my typewriter and typed yet another resumé, one that I could live with and maintain a clear conscience.

This, then, is the resumé that I read to the North Carolina civic club immediately after the program chairman had read the other one:

"TRUE RESUMÉ OF WALKER W. 'BO' WHALEY"

Born in Scott, Georgia, December 11, 1927. His parents took one look and cried out, "No more!" resulting in Bo being raised an only child. His father exclaimed, "My God! He looks like a boll weevil!" Thus, the nickname.

Bo moved with his parents to the small South Georgia

towns of Dudley, Vidette, Alma, Oglethorpe, Lumpkin, and Metter inasmuch as the Foster Parents program had not yet been instituted and they had no choice but to take him along.

In May, 1943, Bo was awarded (and I emphasize the word "awarded") his high school diploma from Stewart County High School, Lumpkin, Georgia, but only after having taken a make-up algebra test in the principal's office three hours before graduation. His grade on the test has never been revealed and went to the grave with the compassionate principal in 1958. A clue surfaced, however, when it was learned that the principal signed Bo's diploma with an "X," possibly to serve as a lifelong reminder that Bo never learned the true value of "X," or "Y" either, for that matter.

By some miracle, and a borrowed $500, Bo's father enrolled him in Georgia Military College, Milledgeville, Georgia (the city in which the Georgia State Mental Hospital is located). It has been long rumored that at the end of the first week the school sent a letter to Bo's father to inquire if, indeed,

he had enrolled his son in the intended institution in Milledgeville.

During the World War II years, anybody with a pulse and $500 could get in college. And as long as the payments kept coming, the only way to get kicked out of a military school was to hold hands on campus with the Cadet Colonel (bear in mind

this was a long time ago and times have changed) or make a pass at the Commandant's wife. Incidentally, these are the only two subjects Bo passed his freshman year.

While at GMC, Bo played varsity football, basketball, baseball, and track. This is not surprising, however, as all the real athletes were in the armed forces playing throw the grenade, drop the bomb, or shoot the Japs and Germans. Also, Bo was named Most Outstanding Athlete both years he attended GMC, but only after climbing the fire escape in his shorts after midnight bed check, entering the athletic office, and stuffing the ballot box, thereby also qualifying for the gymnastics team.

Bo fought like hell during World War II, but the authorities caught up with him and sent him overseas anyway, to the South Pacific where he had the dual dangerous assignments of operating the movie projector at night and playing on the baseball team in Manila by day.

After being discharged in November, 1946, and with nothing better to do—the GI Bill money and Georgia Southern College girls look-ing good—Bo decided to enroll, and did, in January, 1947. He was on the baseball and basketball teams there, primarily because he owned an automobile—a rarity in 1947—and that's the way the team traveled back in those days. Had he somehow managed to lose his driver's license, there is little doubt that his name would have been deleted from the traveling squad.

Two years, three girls, and 4,000 laughs later, Bo graduated in June, 1949. Looking for the easy way out as usual, he returned to the scene of the crime and joined the GMC faculty as basketball coach and history teacher. After all, being as stingy as he was, where else but a military school could he work in those old Army uniforms? He resigned after two years when he had exhausted all valid and acceptable excuses for losing.

Possessing no real desire to work, Bo opted to again climb aboard the federal gravy train and enrolled at George Peabody College, in Nashville, Tennessee, on what was left of his GI Bill. As he sat in the registrar's office, the dean eyed him suspiciously and asked, "What course do you wish to pursue?" Bo eyed a framed document on the wall behind the dean's desk and replied, "I want one of them."

Sure enough, a year and 52 Grand Ole Oprys later, the college surrendered and gave him one, a Master of Education degree just like the one hanging on the wall in the registrar's office.

In September, 1951, Bo put on a coat and tie, shaved, borrowed some deodorant and fifty dollars, and rode his motorcycle to Dublin, Georgia, to apply for the position of basketball coach at Dublin High School. The school superintendent, a basketball fan, hired him in a weak moment.

Bo fooled 'em in Dublin for three years until Uncle Sam rescued him and appointed him as a Special Agent of the FBI, after obviously failing to recruit a sufficient number of qualified applicants to fill the October, 1954, new agent's class.

What the heck, he'd try anything once. He did, and for the next 21 years toured the country with a gold badge, a .38 caliber revolver, a Navy blue suit, white shirt, conservative tie, and a snap brim hat—a Hoover man.

In 1972 Bo became an activist in the Women's Liberation Movement, liberating one in Divorce Court, and for the next few years sort of drifted. Well, really, he was a bum, cruising solo in the single lane on life's freeway.

Finally, in January, 1978, Bo moved back to Dublin, Georgia, the best of more than forty moves he's made, when a longtime friend posed the question, "How about writing a column for the *Courier Herald* three times a week?"

Bo said, "Why not?" And now, 1700 columns later, that's where he hangs his snap brim hat and props his Western boots on a desk.

And that, friends and neighbors, is the way the cotton pickin' resumé should have been written in the first place.

YES, YOU CAN LOVE YANKEES WITH A CLEAR CONSCIENCE

I'm not about to turn out the night light and put this book to bed without elaborating on the fifteen years I spent in Michigan, New Jersey, and New York. These years represent one-fourth of my life.

I'm convinced that there are good people in all of America's fifty states, and I can't say enough about the good things that happened to me in Yankeeland. In a sense I am a survivor, a survivor because of some select Yankees who took me by the hand and guided me over the rough spots like language, food, and customs.

I literally slid into Michigan on a snowy December night in 1955, void of things like snow tires, chains, galoshes, rubber boots, overcoat, earmuffs, and everything else associated with ice, snow, and cold weather. What I knew about snow and ice you could have written on an OCB cigarette paper and had room left over. But I learned quickly.

I learned even more when I was transferred from Detroit to Marquette, Michigan, in October, 1960. I remember the date well: October 19, 1960. Check the weather reports for that date and you'll find that Marquette had a seventeen-inch snowfall that night, and sixteen inches more the next day! That's pretty heavy for a South Georgia boy. And my house was three miles outside of Marquette on the shores of Lake Superior. I survived that first Marquette winter in Michigan's Upper Peninsula only because of the kindness and compassion of a Yankee, Leo Glass.

Leo owned a junkyard in Marquette, but he also owned something else—a snowmobile. Every morning following a heavy snowfall the night before, Leo would arrive at my house early on his snowmobile with such necessities as milk, eggs, bacon, coffee, and the like. To this day I'm convinced he saved my life, as well as the lives of my wife and children.

Leo Glass is but one of the many friends I made while living in Yankeeland, and the more I consider the years I spent up there, the more I'm convinced that it really is impossible to love or hate anybody unless you know them. And to get to know them, you must live with them, laugh with them, cry with them, and come to realize that we all share the same concerns. We just talk about them with different accents.

Never in my life have I ever known the beauty of nature more intimately than I came to know it in Michigan, New Jersey, and New York. These are beautiful states, with picture-post-card scenes at every turn. Any artist would have a field day in them. And the people are good people, people who share the same feelings and emotions in the North that we share in Dixie. They center around family, church, and education for their children. So what if some of their customs differ from those down here? Wouldn't ours be a boring and drab existence if we all thought and lived alike?

I cherish the years I spent north of the Mason-Dixon Line, the friends I made there, and the great memories I have of the area. I can state right here and now— without reservations—that I can and do love Yankees with a clear conscience.